The
War in the Trenches

Alan Lloyd

The War in the Trenches

General Editor:
Ludovic Kennedy

David McKay Company, Inc.,
New York

First American Edition, 1976

Library of Congress Catalog Card Number: 76–41567
ISBN 0–679–50716–7

Printed in Great Britain by
William Clowes & Sons, Limited
London, Beccles and Colchester

Contents

Acknowledgements

The photographs and illustrations in this book are reproduced by kind permission of the following. Those on pages 17, 19, 22, 25, 26–7, 28, 32, 34, 35, 36, 37, 38–9, 40, 46, 48, 53, 55, 57, 60–61, 66, 71, 73, 74–5, 76, 80, 82, 90–91, 93, 96–7, 98, 100, 102, 104, 106–7, 109, 112, 114, 117, 118–19, 120, 122–3, 124, 128–9, 130, 132–3, 134–5, 136–7, 144–5, 147, 148–9, 150, 152, 155, 157, 159, 160, 162, 164, 166, 173, 174–5, 176, 177, 179, 180, 182, 184–5, 186, 189, Imperial War Museum; pages 10, 12, 51, 85, 140, 142, 190, 193, Mansell Collection; pages 44, 64–5, Professor B. Howell; page 8, The Tate Gallery; page 18, National Army Museum; page 176, The Royal Leicestershire Regiment; page 13, Musée du Château de Versailles; page 143, Etablissement Cinématographique des Armées. Illustration Research Service and Celia Dearing supplied the pictures. The maps were drawn by Brian and Constance Dear.

Introduction

For many of England's young men the outbreak of the 1914 war seemed a romantic adventure, an opportunity for winning honour and glory – 'as swimmers', Rupert Brooke saw them, 'into cleanness leaping'. Four years later, after millions of young Englishmen, Frenchmen and Germans had perished on the muddy battlefields of the Somme and the Aisne and Passchendaele, the war was recognized for what it was: one of the bloodiest and most futile conflicts in history.

It was also the most immobile war ever fought. For weeks, sometimes months on end, the two sides faced each other across the narrow strip of No Man's Land – often so near that they could hear each other talking. They lived in crude dug-outs that were seldom free of water, they were plagued by trench fever and trench feet; and they knew that at almost any moment their lives might be snuffed out by a shell or a sniper's bullet.

At length one side or other decided to attack. There would be hours of nerve-racking bombardment, mines exploding under enemy trenches and blowing the occupants sky-high, sometimes gas too; then the attackers would climb out of their trenches and advance, *often at walking pace*, towards the enemy lines. They were mown down in their thousands. Winston Churchill called 'fighting machine-guns with the breasts of gallant men'. In one day on the Somme the British lost fifty-seven thousand men; and for every man killed, there were at least three others maimed.

Those who survived trench warfare rarely spoke of it afterwards. It was too unique and too terrible to convey to others. But in the creased faces of those very old men who march so proudly to Church on Remembrance Sunday, you can still see something of the suffering and comradeship they shared.

Ludovic Kennedy

Chapter 1

The Soldiers

Summer, 1914. Europe, still regarding electric light, the telephone and the motor van as novelties, lurched towards another innovation: the first great war of the twentieth century. In seventy years Germany had risen from a score of minor principalities to become the most powerful state in the world. Her neighbours were fearful. Neither France nor Russia was a match for the central giant, and when prudence forged their alliance, Germany in turn chafed.

Many tensions heightened the mutual fear: intense nationalistic passions, the disturbing swell of new technology, the idiosyncrasies of dominating men, including the unstable William of Hohenzollern, third Kaiser of the German Reich.

One incident, and Europe would reach for its weaponry. It came in June. Six years earlier, Germany's declining ally, Austria, had annexed part of Serbia (now Jugoslavia). Bitterness had lingered. As Austria's unpopular Archduke Francis Ferdinand belatedly drove to inspect his gains, he was shot in the town of Sarajevo. A month later, on 28 July, Austria declared war on Serbia. Russia backed the Slav cause. The great powers rushed to mobilize.

Combined, the manpower resources of France and Russia were formidable but German strength was better organized. Russia suffered from corruption and incompetence in her leadership, industrial backwardness, and insufficient railways to deploy her masses effectively. France could call on four million reservists, as many as Germany, but only 1,500,000 were reckoned of the first line; their weapons were poor, their methods more romantic than practical. The French army possessed two outstanding assets: the quick-firing 75 mm field gun and great élan. The extent of its dependence on them was unreasonable.

Germany produced reservists on the same conscription basis – every able-bodied man did military service – but training and organization were more thorough. Reservist units proved their fitness to fight efficiently at short notice. Surprised opponents attributed this readiness to a brutal training system. 'In fact,' wrote the French military attaché in Berlin, 'the soldiers are treated without harshness.'

The German's dedication to martial endeavour reposed in his staunch belief in the grandeur of his nation's destiny, a conviction instilled and disciplined over generations by his leaders. Linked with a high level of executive competence, and the methodical development of light and heavy weapons, this popular impetus to action

Opposite 'La Mitrailleuse' (The Machine-gun) by C. Nevinson.

9

William II, third
Kaiser of the German
Reich.

enabled Germany to strike first, with startling audacity.

Her western strategy, devised by a former chief of the general staff, Count Schlieffen, involved a great swinging blow at Paris through neutral Belgium, flanking the French armies north and west before rolling them back against Switzerland – hopefully, to win the war at a single stroke.

The initial assault on 'little Belgium' brought Britain into conflict on an appealing note. Though not bound by formal treaty to support France, the British had a tacit agreement to provide an expeditionary force should Germany resort to arms. There was also a strong incentive to disrupt what many saw as Germany's mounting trade and maritime threat to the empire. Abusively critical of British imperialism, the Germans had backed the Boers in South Africa, and were suspected of making trouble elsewhere.

Unlike the continental powers, Britain had no system of military conscription. The Royal Navy was her main guarantee of impunity, apart from which she maintained a small regular army, chiefly for the protection and policing of her overseas dependencies. Though unrivalled for sheer professionalism and practical involvement in recent wars, the British army had evolved its skills and armaments in colonial exigencies of a very different scale from *la grande guerre*.

Despite (or perhaps because of) the limitations of such experience, the British people as a whole received their government's declaration of war on Germany, on 4 August, with enthusiasm. Ebullient optimism surrounded the departure to France of the seven regular divisions which constituted the BEF, the British Expeditionary Force. The Germans described its proportions as 'contemptible'. The British, sustained by visions of their empire wars, awaited victory with confidence. It would be, as the slogan had it, 'all over before Christmas'.

By late August, the prediction looked credible, though not exactly as Britain intended. Packed in hundreds of trains, the Kaiser's conscripts had rolled across Germany to the Rhine, disgorged on the borders of Belgium and northern France, then poured west and south in a great flood as Count Schlieffen had preordained. On brawny German horses, in juddering, solid-tyred trucks, on the soles of stout new jack boots, more than a million obedient sons of the Fatherland began their march on Paris.

As the right wing of the German force smashed through Belgium, the French left shuddered and recoiled. The BEF stood at Mons, near the French-Belgian border. It took the impact of the Kaiser's 1st Army with a steadiness far from 'contemptible'. Well positioned, deadly with their volley fire, the British regulars brought the Germans to a bloody halt. 'The rapid and accurate rifle fire to which our men had been trained was an eye-opener to the enemy, and they believed at the time that they were opposed by an enormous number of machine-guns,' wrote a British observer.

But the hold-up was momentary.

Within twenty-four hours, the French left was in full retreat, obliging the BEF to go with it. While the Germans pressed remorselessly in pursuit, the allies struggled back along roads jammed with refugees, horse wagons and ambulances, barely daring to sleep or even pause to rest their legs. For more than a hundred miles the retreat continued until, early in September, the French and British troops turned and stood their ground just north of Paris.

The climactic moment had arrived in the progression of the Schlieffen Plan. One last swing at the apprehensive capital and the

Colonel-General
Helmuth Graf von
Moltke, Chief of the
German General Staff.

heart would be cut from French resistance, the surviving allied forces left without refuge.

But Schlieffen had erred on a vital point. At a time when most army transport was unmechanized, and the heaviest of *materiel* had to be humped by hand, his strategy called in the end for supermen. The German soldier, for all his loyal intent, was only human. Beset by demolitions, guerilla action and precarious supply lines, he had

willed himself forward mile after grinding mile until his jack boots adhered to raw and swollen feet. When it came to the final heave he was exhausted, drained as completely as his enemies.

Colonel-General Helmuth Graf von Moltke, Chief of the German General Staff, had been dubious of Schlieffen's scheme from the first. Now as reports from the distant front confirmed his doubts he covered his face and wept. Far removed from his field

General Joseph Jacques Joffre, Allied Commander-in-Chief.

13

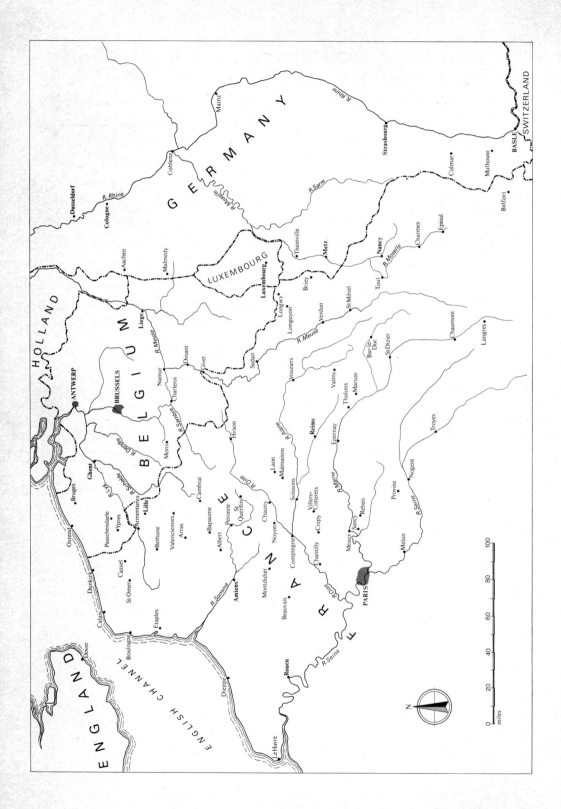

commanders, hampered by the crude communications systems of the day, the sensitive Moltke's problems had increased the nearer his armies got to their objective.

By contrast General Joseph Jacques Joffre, the allied commander-in-chief at Paris, had increased his power. Huge in body and confidence if less so in intellect, Joffre became the dynamic presence, Moltke, the absent authority. On 6 September, Joffre launched his counter-blow at the over-extended German armies by the River Marne. Its momentum was sluggish. Both sides were spent, and a late summer heatwave did not help.

But at last the invasion forces gave ground. The BEF drove doggedly into a gap in the grey line and threatened the German rear. Within thirty miles of triumph the Kaiser's legions reversed, ebbing back to the River Aisne where, in accordance with a last order from the broken Moltke, they entrenched themselves.

To the north the German generals turned their eyes towards the sea in a bid to seize the Channel ports. In October, mounting a fierce attack on the Belgian town of Ypres, they found the BEF again in front of them. The Germans suffered massive casualties, but the little British army was also dwindling and it had no reserves. Cooks, tailors, clerks and transport drivers filled the line. The Royal Field Artillery stood firm, firing over open sights. The line held. With winter setting in, both sides consolidated their positions.

Abortive allied attempts to dislodge the Germans from their entrenchments on the Aisne had taught the French a lesson. General Ferdinand Foch, co-ordinating allied operations in the north, spread the message: 'You must dig in; it's the only way of staying out of sight and cutting losses.' As rain fell, and movement was curtailed by sticky ground, the theme was taken up everywhere until a continuous line of opposed trenches snaked from neutral Switzerland, across France, to the Belgian coast.

The war of movement was over.

Though on a scale and at a cost which evidenced the unprecedented destructiveness of modern conflict (the BEF's casualties reached eighty-six thousand by the year's end, the majority in the first three months; French and German losses were many times greater), still it had essentially been war in the old style. Ahead lay something different: a confrontation in which massed forces went to earth; in which the foe, though always near, was seldom seen; in which death struck invisibly and unannounced. Such was the new face of battle – the trench war.

Map 1 opposite The Western Front, 1914–18.

The first British troops embroiled in the trench war were regulars of the original BEF, the self-styled 'Old Contemptibles'. Among the millions of men deployed in 1914, they were highly distinctive. Largely concerned until the outbreak of hostilities with empire security, a duty involving long and lonely stints in distant parts, Britain's diminutive professional army had developed a self-sufficient and insular attitude scarcely cognizant of the civilian world.

Wrote a soldier of the period:

> The army carried its own life with it wherever it went, and you lived pretty much the same, whether you were in India, China, or any other place. You lived between the barrack-room and the wet canteen, without any social life at all. For all the years I was in India before the war, I was never in a house ... There was a ritual every evening. The men would make themselves absolutely spotless – uniform pressed, boots polished, hair plastered down – as if every one of them had a girl-friend waiting at the gate. But they had no girl-friends, and they never went out of the gate. They went straight down to the wet canteen and got drunk. That was what they got dressed up for. (C.S.M. Robert Leggat, Scottish Rifles.)

It was a hard life. Discipline was harsh, pay was modest (a shilling a day for the private, with an extra sixpence for gaining special shooting proficiency) and an obsession with 'spit and polish' left few really free hours.

But it inculcated a powerful regimental camaraderie. Many of the recruits came from deprived social backgrounds. In place of squalor, poverty and rejection, the regular army gave them cleanliness, security and acceptance. The result was often profound. Readiness to die for the regiment, though not something men talked about, was more than an idle cliché.

Promotion was hard earned. On average, it took a man four years to gain the rank of lance-corporal, eight to become a corporal, and twelve to reach sergeant. Sergeants and warrant officers messed separately from the lower ranks, forming a select society ruled absolutely by the regimental sergeant-major, the authority most responsible for the daily routine and discipline of unit life. The sergeants' mess, with its games nights, occasional dances and heavy drinking, was the dynamo of the regiment. Officers, though sometimes invited, lived in yet another world.

Many regular officers, especially those of the élite brigades and cavalry units, were wealthy men, and all regiments demanded minimum levels of private income from officers joining them. When a 2nd lieutenant's pay was about £100 a year, some cavalry regi-

ments expected him to have £1,000 a year of his own, the Cold-stream Guards insisted on £400, a typical county regiment might have advised £200.

There was plenty to spend it on. Unavoidable mess bills alone topped the pay of a subaltern. Uniform, purchased at his own expense, was costly. Apart from full dress, patrol dress, mess dress, service dress and field service dress an officer needed well cut plain clothes and all manner of sporting togs and equipment.

Sartorial elegance was more than a fancy. An aspiring young officer could go a long way on appearance, especially if it was supported by a couple of good hunters and a few polo ponies.

The officers' mess was a club run on strict and hierarchical rules. A subaltern might be forbidden to open conversation with a senior officer until he had been six months with the regiment; rank might

Tank officers relax in camp at Poperinghe, 1917.

Opposite Set of Wills Cigarette recruiting cards.

govern who was, or was not, entitled to warm his backside at the ante-room hearth. Mess kit was *de rigueur* for dinner, dinner jacket for supper, and so on. Some regiments even stipulated the brand of cigarettes to be smoked by their officers.

Such emphasis on 'form' and petty ritual heightened the sense of belonging and exclusiveness which went right through the army. It was held, and the record did not disprove it, to provide the regular soldier with a degree of pride and identity which sustained him in battle.

Actual tactical training was fairly crude, based on rudimentary 'fire and movement' precepts. But the British infantryman, adroit with his ·303 Lee Enfield rifle (a weapon so efficient that it survived World War II in standard use), was a superb attacking soldier. The artillery, horse-drawn, moved with panache and was brisk into action, while the cavalry regiments, the pride of the generals, idealized the spirit of the whole force in their role of pursuit and harassment. Accustomed to world commuting, equally at home in brilliant ceremonial, fighting like dogs or enduring prolonged boredom without complaint, the British regular army was a unique institution.

The departure of the BEF to France denuded Britain of her professional troops. Battalions serving in Empire stations were hastily ordered home, only to be sent straight to the continent. Meanwhile the single military reserve left in the island was the volunteer Territorial Force. Composed of part-time soldiers trained in their spare hours, the Territorial Force was keen, generally proficient, and replete to the strength of fourteen infantry divisions and as many brigades of yeomanry (cavalry).

These were promptly mobilized full time for home defence, their intended role. It proved a fleeting one. Almost immediately the need for reinforcements on the continent threw the Territorials into the front line. Legally they were not liable for service overseas, but few refused when asked to join the BEF.

Now, as the high losses of the early weeks clouded initial complacency, the home shores were drained entirely of trained men. Nobody could deny that more troops were needed, but the new war minister, Field-Marshal Lord Kitchener, saw the need in terms which startled many. While most military authorities contemplated reinforcing the existing martial structure, Kitchener demanded a completely new army. Moreover, he projected his requirements not on the basis of a swift victory but in the expectation of a fierce conflict running into three years.

To the consternation of the War Office, Kitchener set out to create seventy divisions in this period. Pessimists saw it as fantasy. Where were the officers, the n.c.o.s, the training staffs? Every real soldier the nation possessed was already at the front, or on his way there. Kitchener's army would be a rabble of civilians, declared the traditionalists – *kannonenfutter*, as the Germans confidently observed when they heard of the plan.

In late August, Kitchener made his celebrated appeal for the 'First Hundred Thousand' men. Coinciding with news of the BEF's retreat on Paris, it produced a surge of emotional response throughout the country. For the average Briton of the time, patriotism still ranked as a cardinal virtue, like honesty or cleanliness. The nation's power in the world, together with her touchingly modest proportions and the natural beauties of the island (yet unspoilt by the motor car and rampant industry), held people in simple thrall. The middle classes, and a significant proportion of the lower classes, enjoyed a sense of comfort and security which they were prepared to preserve staunchly against any threat.

'Now, God be thanked, who has matched us with this hour,' wrote a young middle class Englishman, Rupert Brooke, whose poem 'The Soldier' captured for many the essence of a country well worth dying for:

> Her sights and sounds; dreams happy as her day;
> And laughter learnt of friends; and gentleness,
> In hearts at peace, under an English heaven.

If it was a heaven of less obvious charm for the numerous poor and underprivileged, their patriotism was perhaps the more remarkable. While they shared few of the material benefits of Empire, at least Britain's far-flung connections opened visions to them of distant peoples whose lot in life seemed even more unpalatable than their own. No Briton was so deprived that he could not swell with superiority at soldiers' tales, popularly exploited in pulp fiction, of the poor benighted heathen of the colonies. Born of ignorance, fed by romantic propaganda, an incorrigible if amiable condescension towards all foreigners bolstered the pride of the neediest Briton in 1914.

Other motives besides patriotism spurred enlistment, among them an urge to break the parochial limits which circumscribed the experience of many young men; a widespread weariness with

the drudgery of ill paid jobs; a longing to escape the drabness of slum life. For one reason or another the men of Britain answered Kitchener's call by crowding improvised recruiting stations in numbers which confounded all predictions.

For many, the gesture was surprisingly spontaneous.

'One morning,' recalled an early volunteer, 'I left home to go to work: we were repairing roads at the time, but on the way I met a friend who was going to enlist. Instead of going on to work, I went back home, changed into my best clothes and went with him to the recruiting office.'

Similar instances were innumerable. So many men wanted to soldier with schoolmates, workmates or clubmates, that sizeable units were formed on this basis. A city tramways department filled a battalion within sixteen hours of opening its recruiting office. The clerks and warehousemen of Manchester formed a battalion, as did the Glasgow 'commercials', the assorted sportsmen of Hull, and scores of other social groups. Eventually, these new units were attached to county regiments, but for a long time they retained the affection of their members as so-called 'pals' or 'chums' battalions.

Youngsters were particularly anxious to volunteer. Countless youths falsified birth dates to meet the official minimum age of nineteen. Not uncommonly, the authorities abetted them or turned a blind eye. A sixteen-year-old recruit later recounted an experience familiar to thousands: 'The recruiting sergeant asked me my age and when I told him he said, "You had better go out, come in again, and tell me different." I came back, told him I was nineteen and I was in.'

The War Office was astonished by the flood of recruitment. Within three weeks, half a million men had volunteered. The New Army had been born.

But its problems were formidable. Without officers, without n.c.o.s, without uniforms, guns or tents, Kitchener's multitudinous infant sprawled across the country, seeking shelter as best it could. *Opposite* Women of Barns and railway carriages became barrack rooms. Some men Britain say 'GO!' went back at night to their own homes. Reception centres were chaotic. Recruits reported using tin cans from scrap heaps for drinking mugs, and scooping up stew in their bare hands.

The situation called for direct methods, and Kitchener encouraged them. Ranks were allocated with a simplicity which horrified the military establishment. Typically, one new battalion was met at its depot by a junior lieutenant who immediately appealed for anyone who had ever been in charge of other men, or who might care to be. When about forty recruits stepped forward, 23 white tape was tied round their arms and they were proclaimed lance-corporals.

Commanders were provided by recalling elderly soldiers from retirement – often veterans of Victorian campaigns – or by withholding a few protesting regular officers from their battalions. For the rest, commissions were allocated almost as haphazardly as were non-commissioned ranks. To most generals, the notion of an officer not qualified by Sandhurst training was appalling. But a dozen Sandhursts could not cope with the requirements. Clinging to some vestige of their standards the generals stipulated that, so far as possible, commissions should go to recruits educated at public schools.

Public school men were not always interested. There was considerable enthusiasm for the 'gentleman ranker's' life. One battalion was raised entirely from former public school boys who preferred to serve in the ranks. More significantly, as it would transpire, those who did take commissions were mostly far removed in outlook and ambition from regular officers. To the bemusement of the generals, they became, as R. C. Sherriff, who enlisted in 1914, put it, 'leaders in a totally different way'.

At first, indeed, a scarcely convincing way. Supervised by antediluvian commanders, spared little attention by contemporary regulars, raw young officers muddled through the early weeks with at least the consolation that the rookies beneath them knew no better. A distinct suggestion of the blind leading the blind pervaded the nation's training camps.

In one unexceptional division, no more than fourteen of well over four hundred officers had any military experience. But, gradually, the novices found their feet. As the improvised uniforms and dummy guns first issued gave way to proper equipment, the officers and men of Kitchener's army began to acquire the feel of soldiering.

Everywhere, the countryside reverberated to the clump of drill boots and the bawdy chant of marching songs. Field and heath swarmed with pallid city denizens manoeuvring in accordance with training manual regulations. Inevitably, square-bashing was prevalent. 'On three mornings a week,' wrote a Kitchener subaltern, 'we marched our companies about on the parade ground in massed formations as though we were preparing to fight in the Marlborough wars. On other mornings we practised in open formations for the Boer War.'

One omission was glaring, in retrospect.

'We were not taught how to fight in trenches. These, we were

24

told, were merely a temporary phase. In the spring, when our new armies were ready, we would break out of the trench line and chase the Germans back to the Rhine.'

Wheeled stretcher operating behind the trenches in dry period.

Meanwhile training, in green and open parts, with its spirit of adventure and companionship, provided a novel and happy interlude between the dull routine left behind and the unknown ordeal ahead. 'Who of all those who were in camp at the time and are still alive, will not remember until he dies the second boyhood that he had in the late frosts and then in the swiftly filling and bursting spring?' asked C. E. Montague, a Kitchener volunteer. Young men who had in many cases scarcely stepped outside the slums of their birth, awoke for the first time to bird song, experienced the spacious peace of a rural evening, relished haversack rations munched amid buttercups.

It was a short-lived awakening. As 1915 progressed the mood of the New Army subtly changed. The batches of wounded returning

from the Western Front and the growing number of families touched
by bereavement gradually spread the realization that training and
fighting were different things.

So many men had responded to Kitchener's appeals – about
two million by the final count – that the volunteers were no longer
a special and fêted group. Young men who had *not* joined up were
more conspicuous. Misguided women sent them white feathers. Of
necessity recruiting became less a matter of entreaty, more a matter

of pressure, and there was talk of conscription. Britain had never before contemplated such a step.

Thus, in a humour still dominated by eagerness to prove themselves, to show the Kaiser what Britons were made of, yet now qualified by the imminence of danger, the initial divisions of Kitchener's army completed their training and prepared for embarkation. The men expected hardship and sacrifice. They were not prepared for the trenches, but that's what they got.

The grim face of the trench war: a German dug-out with former occupant.

27

Chapter 2

Entrenchment

Though Germany's attempt to knock out France with a single blow had failed in 1914, Moltke's thrust had resulted in striking gains. So deep were the Germans into enemy territory by winter that on much of the front they could afford to discard poorly defensible ground and consolidate on the strongest line.

The allies on the other hand counted every yard. The Belgians, along a few vital miles in the far north, and the French, holding a front of several hundred miles to the south, itched to expel the invaders without delay.

The British, too, fretted to go forward. Dug in between their partners – south from Ypres towards the Somme river – the BEF was unpleasantly conscious of the sea lapping at its back. The compulsion to seize ground, strong in the allied camp, resulted generally in works of a less permanent nature than the enemy's, and often of inferior location.

Standard British entrenchment consisted of three lines: a forward line protected by barbed wire entanglements, machine-gun nests and listening posts; a support line; and a reserve line. Each trench was cut in a continuous pattern of traverses; that is, short legs or bays zigzagging at right angles to reduce the possible effect of enfilade or shell blast.

Viewed from the air, the impression was of a castellated design curiously symbolic of the medieval siege warfare in which this new form of confrontation could trace some early origins.

The infantry, threading the traverses like khaki skeins, was organized basically as follows: at the centre was the ordinary 'Tommy', the private soldier. On either side of him were the mates of his section, the nuclear infantry group of about a dozen fighting men headed by a corporal. Each section was part of a platoon of four sections, led by a lieutenant with the help of a sergeant.

Four platoons formed the fighting strength of an infantry company which, with various administrative and specialist personnel, ran to some 240 men, nominally commanded by a major (though not infrequently, when officers were short, by a captain). Next came the battalion. The battalion, representing its parent the regiment, was commanded by a lieutenant-colonel and comprised at full strength thirty-six officers and a thousand men, though its actual fighting strength (four rifle companies) was nearer eight hundred. Twelve battalions (three brigades) were incorporated in the largest unit of permanent components involved in the trench war, the infantry division.

Opposite A sentry on the fire-step of a snow-covered trench near Roclincourt.

29

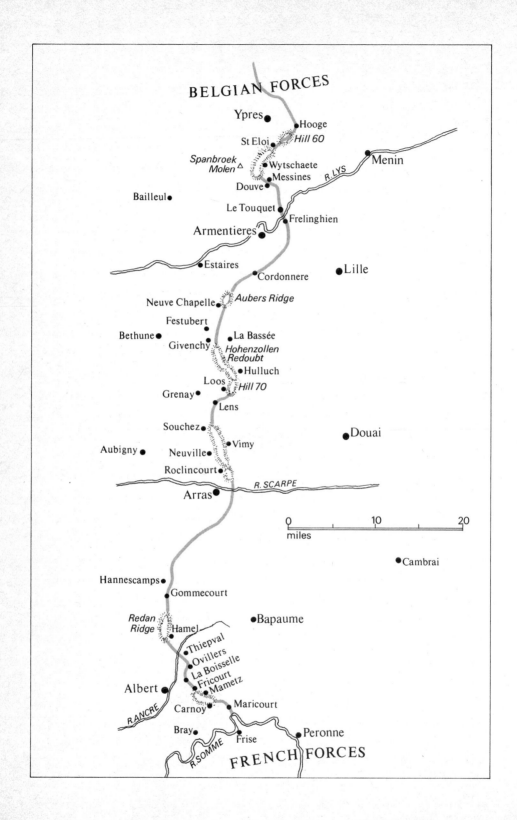

BELGIAN FORCES

Ypres ●
● Hooge
St Eloi ● ✶ *Hill 60*
Spanbroek △ ● Wytschaete   ● Menin
Molen   Messines
Douve ●   *R. LYS*
Bailleul ●
Le Touquet ●
   ● Frelinghien
Armentieres ●

● Estaires
   ● Cordonnere   ● Lille

Neuve Chapelle ● ✶ *Aubers Ridge*
Festubert ●
Bethune ●   ● La Bassée
Givenchy ● ✶ *Hohenzollen*
   Redoubt
   ● Hulluch
Loos ● ✶ *Hill 70*
Grenay ●
   ● Lens
Souchez ●
   ● Vimy   ● Douai
Aubigny ●   Neuville ●
Roclincourt ●
   R. SCARPE
Arras ●

0   10   20
miles

● Cambrai

Hannescamps ●
  Gommecourt ●
Redan ✶
Ridge ● Hamel   ● Bapaume
   ● Thiepval
   ● Ovillers
   ● La Boisselle
   ● Fricourt
Albert ●   ● Mametz
  R. ANCRE   ● Maricourt
  Carnoy ●
Bray ●   ● Frise   ● Peronne
  R. SOMME

FRENCH FORCES

The major-general commanding a division might be responsible for several miles of line. About half his full establishment of almost twenty thousand men were rifle troops; others manned machine guns and field guns. Apart from infantrymen, the division contained companies of Royal Field Artillery, Royal Engineers and a staff of Royal Army Medical Corps personnel.

The engineers were responsible for supervising trench works and for signal communications. Horses demanded much attention. In the early days of the BEF, motor haulage was practically unknown (at the last moment, a few brewery lorries had been commandeered, but the supply of spare parts was inadequate) and it took the labours of more than five thousand horses to keep an infantry division in the field.

British trenches were virtually large ditches. In places they might have been deep enough to provide full cover for a standing man but the sides were generally heightened by a parapet of sandbags. In order to shoot over the top the troops mounted a fire-step. Sometimes the Germans were entrenched so near that their voices could be heard from the British lines. Still, the most intimate and persistent enemy of the trench soldier, particularly in winter, was privation. 'Nothing to see but bare mud walls,' complained one occupant; 'nowhere to sit but on a wet muddy ledge; no shelter of any kind against the weather except the clothes you are wearing; no exercise you can take in order to warm yourself.'

Rain was the greatest curse. When the clouds burst, the trenches became dykes. Icy water, submerging duckboards, rose to ankle, knee, even thigh depth. Long periods of immersion caused the men's feet to swell until keeping their boots on was torture, while taking them off produced worse results, for they could not then be replaced.

'The excruciating agonies and misery through which the men had to go in those days before anti-"trench feet" measures were taken were unimaginable,' recalled an officer of the first winter. Thousands suffered before gumboots were sparingly issued.

Map 2 opposite BEF operations, 1915–17.

At night, soaked puttees and trousers froze stiff while the troops huddled in holes scraped in the trench walls. Officers and senior n.c.o.s occupied larger holes known as dug-outs.

'Here I was in this horrible clay cavity,' wrote one officer of his initiation to trench life, 'cold, wet through and covered with mud. Nothing was to be heard except the occasional crack of the sniper's shot, the dripping of rain, and the low murmur of voices from the outer cave. In the narrow space beside me lay my equipment: revolver and sodden packet of cigarettes. Everything was damp, 31

cold and dark; candle guttering ... the Boche is just on the other side of the field and there doesn't seem the slightest chance of leaving except in an ambulance.'

The writer, a young lieutenant named Bruce Bairnsfather, duly left the trenches as anticipated, the victim of a German shell.

From his early experiences Bairnsfather was inspired to create one of the best known cartoon characters of the war, Old Bill, the archetypal trench dweller. Hunched like a comatose night watch-man in his shapeless great-coat and 'Balaclava', Old Bill was chiefly remarkable as the antithesis of the immaculate regular soldier of pre-war days, an ironic comment on the common destiny of all troops consigned to the trenches.

For millions in Britain Bairnsfather's phlegmatic troglodyte brought a smile to the trench war. At least he had his pipe and the battered bucket which served as a brazier.

But in the early days of entrenchment even these simple comforts were frowned on. Smoking or the lighting of fires for warmth and cooking were held to jeopardize positions, as if the men were scouting in the Transvaal. Later, as long immobility bound the opposed lines with familiarity, restrictions were relaxed. Where the trenches were close, British and German troops sometimes joined voice in evening sing-songs, and at Christmas 1914 actually met in No Man's Land to exchange souvenirs.

'It was like the interval between rounds in a boxing match,' reported a participant. 'Our men in their scratch costumes of dirty, muddy khaki, with their various head-dresses of woollen helmets, mufflers and battered hats [steel helmets were not introduced to the British army until 1916] ... the Huns in their grey-green faded uniforms, top boots and pork-pie hats. ... Everyone was talking, laughing and souvenir hunting.'

More normally, trench life followed a daily routine of bleak discomfort.

Shortly before first light, the men manned the fire-step in case the enemy mounted a dawn attack. After this procedure, known as 'stand-to', breakfast was cooked on coke fires, the troops washed and shaved as best they could, then performed minor chores. On a quiet day, there was time enough for rest and boredom, but relaxation was difficult. Runners were constantly trudging past with messages, n.c.o.s thought up odd jobs, various officers dropped by to inspect the lines. Dusk brought a repeat of the morning stand-to, and hot food was brought forward from the field kitchens. With luck, rum was issued. Each soldier was entitled to a tot a day though not all commanders agreed to its issue, some fearing it might impair vigilance.

Opposite 'The Price of a Pint' – an Old Bill cartoon by Bruce Bairnsfather.

British and German troops fraternize, Christmas, 1914.

Night was the time of major activity. Troop and supply movements to and from the trenches were carried out under cover of darkness, as were repairs to dug-outs, sandbagging, wire entanglements and so forth. Gingerly, patrols and spying sorties ventured towards the enemy, probing for weaknesses in their defences. Periodically the Germans sent up flares, and the scouts would hold their breath while machine guns swept No Man's Land.

In fact violent action intruded for relatively short spells on trench life. But the threat of danger, with its attendant tensions, was constant. Violence had an unnerving habit of arriving unexpectedly, allowing scope neither for evasion nor retaliation. Sniper fire was much feared, in this category.

The German sniper operated for long spells in one location, learning every wrinkle of a British trench. With telescopic sights on his rifle, he became adept at picking off careless occupants or those who for reasons of duty were constrained to take risks. Look-outs peered cautiously through small gaps between sandbags; nevertheless, so many look-outs were shot through the head in the early days that some units purchased or improvised periscopes at their own initiative. In time these surveillance devices were issued officially.

Opposite 'Daddy, what did you do in the Great War?'

Where the lines were close, grenades were another menace. The German grenade, with a throwing handle, could be hurled a disconcerting distance by a powerful and practised arm. More devastating was the *Minnenwerfer*, a German mortar projecting a large explosive canister packed with metal fragments.

34   Liable to strike without warning at the quietest times, these

Daddy, what did _YOU_ do in the Great War?

G.H.Q.
30th May 1917
ORPEN

Comparative luxury of a German dug-out, Argonne, 1915.

dangers were a persistent threat in the trenches. Still, the most dreaded phenomena in the minds of all trench soldiers were the sudden artillery bombardments which tore earthworks and occupants apart in a deafening frenzy of savagery – when, as Alec Waugh wrote from experience, 'the shells hailed down so fast that you could not distinguish individual trajectories; when there would be a roar at one side or another and a fountain of earth and iron tossed in a high cascade; when the stretcher bearers were fewer than their tasks.'

For the man in the line, there was no recourse in such fury but to cringe and pray. The gunner on both sides had the trench soldier at his mercy, but the preponderance of heavy guns held by the Germans made their bombardments a special threat. The explosive punches of their big weapons became known by the British troops as 'Jack Johnsons', after the American heavyweight boxer of that name. A lighter German shell, notorious for bursting without the preceding whistle of the 'Jack Johnson', was nicknamed the 'Whizz Bang'.

Since the Germans determinedly responded to British artillery initiatives by pounding the British trenches, the soldiers in them took a poor view of inductive action by their own guns.

Their superiors were less reluctant to make a stir. To the eager commander, trained for warfare of a different tempo, inertia was invidious. Worse, lack of aggression in the proximity of the enemy – a live and let live attitude among the troops – once condoned might become habitual. The fraternization at Christmas had quickly been

Opposite Field-Marshal Sir Douglas Haig, KT, GCB, GCVO, KCIE.

37

condemned by British generals, and a number of the participants court-martialled.

One method of sustaining aggression and working off tension was the custom widely known as 'morning hate'. Staged at the dawn stand-to, when ammunition was plentiful, this noisy exhibition of hostility involved a general exchange of small-arms fire between

the trenches. 'Every man who had ammunition seemed to join in a great wave of shooting across No Man's Land, which swelled up and travelled along the line for ten minutes or a quarter of an hour, then died down,' recalled an infantry officer. It was, he pronounced, 'a strange and unforgettable performance'.

The ritual was largely bloodless. While the men held to the

Night sky, Western Front.

39

Australian dug-out
with wood and steel
supports.

trenches, rifle and machine-gun fire mostly passed overhead, spin-
ning and ricocheting into the distance.

Though at the quietest of periods men trickled away from a
typical battalion at the rate of seven or eight a week killed or
wounded, at least as many were lost through sickness as by German
action. Despite the moments of explosion and terror, the trenches
themselves often seemed, that winter, the worst enemy.

Alternating with trench duty on a roughly equal basis (in spells
of up to about a week), life in billets a few miles to the rear produced
its own miseries. Drill sessions and endless fatigues were much
resented, especially the filling of sandbags, which the infantryman
was never done with. One private, expressing a popular grievance,
wrote that he had enlisted to save France, not to shovel it into sacks.

For all of which, there were some consolations. Many of the towns
and villages behind the lines were charming places, scarcely

touched by the neighbouring tide of war, and there were hours to be snatched in friendly homes and *estaminets*.

Unfortunately for the many who yearned for female company, local girls were considerably outnumbered by soldiery, and bestowed their companionship reservedly. For some troops brothels were an answer, but the proportion of BEF men who used them was not great. The average young officer of the day, reared in a sexually repressive ethos and uneasy with women, was deterred by a mixture of fear and guilt. The ranker did not have the money.

Assuming he sent half his pay home to help the family (a common practice in the army) the private soldier was left with less than four shillings a week from his basic rate to spread between smokes, drink, edible 'luxuries', postcards, gifts for Blighty and such other small extras as he might desire.

Before long the position of the British soldier seeking to impress continental girls was rendered even less viable by competition from dominions troops earning several times his own pay. Canadians, among the first Empire contingents to arrive in France, were dubbed enviously the 'fucking five bobbers' by Britons on a single bob.

Back in the trenches, wealth was of small account. Shillings did not stop shells and the mud was impartial in its embrace. For the regulars, who still formed the backbone of the British line, the whole business was a rueful sequel to years of spit and polish, and the glory of the old campaigns. For the men of the New Army, who began to arrive at the winter's end, it made the most squalid of slums seem like paradise. But spring was ahead, and morale remained unbroken in the BEF.

Between them, Old Bill and Young Bill had added a trick or two to the repertoire of their trade. They knew a bit about trench warfare. What did their leaders know?

In November 1914, three months after the outbreak of hostilities, Herbert Asquith, prime minister of Britain's Liberal government, belatedly formed a special cabinet committee, the War Council, to direct the war. In this somewhat unwieldy body, predominantly of politicians elected on domestic issues, the new war minister was ill at ease.

As a soldier, it was not in Kitchener's nature to reveal military secrets, as he put it, to gentlemen with whom he was 'barely acquainted'. Nor, had the habit appealed to him, was he gifted 41 with the ability to present plans and strategies clearly in the committee room. Both Kitchener and Asquith possessed resolution, strength and courage, but neither had the brilliance which, in one or the other, might have sparked a powerful partnership.

Too often the War Council's directives expressed the vagueness of groping consensus, while the war minister, happier in his field-marshal's cap, engaged in secretiveness and what to some seemed like arrogance. 'I am put here to conduct a great war,' proclaimed Kitchener. It was not a statement that endeared him to those who shared the responsibility. On the other hand there was much about him – not least the loftiness of manner accentuated by his tall, strong figure and purposeful expression – which inspired confidence.

Almost alone Kitchener had dared to predict an extended war, perhaps of three years, and to plan recruitment accordingly. It would, he foresaw, demand armies of unprecedented magnitude. What he had not envisaged was the form the confrontation would take on the Western Front. Wholesale entrenchment had not struck him as a likelihood.

Exasperatedly, he told Viscount Grey, the foreign minister: 'I don't know what is to be done. This isn't war.'

His bemusement was not exceptional. None of the combatant nations was prepared for trench warfare, though the Germans, having studied siege techniques in the Balkan and Russo-Japanese wars, were less at a loss than the allies. Their entrenchment was more thorough; their armoury more appropriate. If the German army would have liked more heavy guns, mortars, grenades, demolition charges, and so on at the outset, the BEF envied it what it had.

The British army had not developed heavy guns. In January 1915, when a Mr Wilfrid Stokes invented a British mortar, the troops were still resorting to missile projectors botched up from shell cases. For seven months the War Office dithered before placing orders for the weapon. It was also late in the field with a hand grenade. The Mills bomb, its answer to the German stick grenade, was not sent for trial until the end of winter. Meanwhile British soldiers were improvising with explosives packed in jam tins.

The inability of the military authorities to think in terms of a new kind of warfare was marked in the field of armoured vehicles, already feasible, and the one type of weapon which might have pierced trench defences with impunity. Caterpillar tractors had been in use for several years. Enthusiasts, including military engineers, were eager to incorporate tracks on some form of 'land cruiser' which could be driven through wire and over earthworks.

One of the first people to show interest was Winston Churchill, then at the Admiralty. In January 1915, he pressed Kitchener, through Asquith, to authorize experiments. Three months later, the War Office made tests with a trench-crossing tractor, but the general in charge was pessimistic and the project flagged. Later, it was to revive dramatically, but the army command was not mechanically minded and Kitchener expressed little personal faith in tanks.

Kitchener's talent, apposite to a great war, was for organizing armies in mass rather than for the detail of battles and weaponry. In Egypt and South Africa, earlier British successes had owed much to his essentially functional handling of resources. Asked, on the eve of one battle, how he proposed to attack, he had replied characteristically that he had brought an adequate army fifteen hundred miles, overcome all logistical problems, and expected his generals 'to do the rest'.

Now, having achieved the seemingly impossible with the formation of the New Army, his grasp of the conditions ahead of it was dubious.

'Kitchener seemed to me very ignorant of what is being done, and how trenches are attacked, and how bombarded,' wrote a visitor to the War Office in 1915. 'He admitted that the nature of the modern lines of defence was quite new to him, and he said he "felt at sea on the subject".'

The man immediately responsible to Kitchener and the War Council for the conduct of the trench war at its onset was Field-Marshal Sir John French, the original commander of the BEF. A Boer War officer and former Chief of the Imperial General Staff (CIGS), French, white whiskered, stocky and volatile, was sixty-three years old and declining in health. Though he did not get on with Kitchener, he conceded that his lack of technical vision was not unique.

'I cannot help wondering why none of us realized what the modern rifle, the machine gun, motor traction, the aeroplane, and wireless telegraphy would bring about,' French admitted later.

It was not so very curious. Almost all wars, especially those in times of rapid technological development, had produced surprises for generals. Advances in military technique were difficult to conceive, more difficult to practise, in peacetime. Understandably, armies tended to embark on wars in the light of past experience. The German army, for example, had discounted a prototype tank in 1913. The French army's instructions on field fortifications were   43

a decade out of date and, in the words of one of its generals, 'reasoned as if the German artillery ought not to exist'.

The important thing for the British command was to catch up rapidly with the evolutionary tendencies evident by the winter of 1914.

A number of factors militated against this. While the problems of trench warfare were most likely to be solved by engineers and gunners, the British commander and most of his generals were cavalrymen, intellectually remote from the mechanized branches of the army, not to say from civilian expertise. Despite Kitchener's caution, these cavalrymen persisted in the notion of a quick war.

Moltke's offensive had shaken them, but, having finally repulsed it at the Marne, they reasoned that the Germans had shot their bolt; that the enemy was ready for the taking once their own troops had been rested and reinforced.

From this viewpoint, the trenches appeared not as a significant war development but as a tiresome, if necessary, interlude. Come spring the BEF would carve through the German line into open country, where, by bold manoeuvre and assault, the commanders hoped quickly to throw the foe into disarray. The German command did not daunt the British generals. That it had failed to seize Paris was the expected omission of an executive which had not fought a war since 1870. Every British general had first-hand fighting experience, and offensive campaigns were his speciality.

Later opinion denigrated the generals as 'donkeys'. More accurately, perhaps, they belonged in analogy to a stable of thoroughbreds. Fettled on the corn of movement, they itched to set their cavalry (presently consuming large quantities of forage in the rear) to charge and pursuit, to get on with the type of warfare they understood.

Until then the fact that their foot troops had gone to earth struck them as a somewhat humiliating reflection on British initiative. At least, since the senior generals of the BEF occupied châteaux well removed from the trenches, they did not have to wallow in the situation. The day had yet to arrive when the 'top brass' of any army was expected to commune with the soldiery. Kitchener himself, though not an unkind man, was 'never seen to address or even notice a private soldier'.

With few exceptions, army and corps commanders restricted their inspections to battalions resting or training behind the line. One soldier recalled seeing a general only once during a year at the front. 'We were very tired and dirty, and there was something incongruous, almost ludicrous in the sight.' Spruce in well cut tunic,

Opposite The Trench Presser or Bosch Bayonet. Cartoon by W. Heath Robinson.

45

riding breeches and immaculately polished cavalry boots, 'he looked like a man on his way to a fancy-dress party.'

It was only on descending to divisional level that command began to touch the ordinary soldier, and by no means all divisional generals were familiar in the trenches.

Thus, with a huge chasm between the troops and the overlords of the BEF, a personal gulf between the C-in-C and Kitchener, and a further communication problem between Kitchener and the government, it was little wonder that the new mode of confrontation remained a mystery to those planning the war itself. As the quickening hedgerows and orchards of France and Belgium signalled a fresh campaign season, the only legitimate experts on trench warfare were the men in the front line.

Opposite King George V inspects a captured dug-out, 1916. The immaculate turn-out of staff officers struck trench soldiers as bizarre.

Chapter 3

Gas

By the beginning of 1915, Moltke's successor as supreme German commander, the fastidiously elegant General Erich von Falkenhayn, had joined Kitchener in the belief that the war would be a long one. The prompt involvement of Turkey, aligned with the Germanic powers, and soon Italy, turning to the other side, did not diminish his conviction. Nor did the poor showing of Russia, starved of munitions, or a doomed British offensive in the Dardanelles.

The contest would be resolved in the west, by attrition, said Falkenhayn, who developed his resources accordingly. The manufacture and distribution of war supplies had been tackled so comprehensively by German industrialists, particularly the brilliant Walther Rathenau, that by spring the general had an ample munitions flow. To get it quickly to the troops, and to facilitate their own movements, he built military railways along the front. His entrenchments were refined to a standard unheard of in the allied line.

A British officer who visited a captured German dug-out was astonished to find it a spacious chamber, sixty feet by twenty feet, with separate officers' mess, servants' quarters, signal section, and so on. The walls were actually recessed to take beds for six officers. Many of these works, as much as forty feet below ground, were built to hold a platoon of men, with rows of bunk beds and alcoves for their equipment.

Tunnels led from the dug-outs to the trenches, which were up to ten feet deep, and to villages just behind the German line, where cellars and ruined buildings were turned into strong posts. Machine-gun nests, the killer teeth in the defence scheme, were sometimes of concrete or steel plate. Hand-picked and well trained, the German machine-gunner could scythe down targets a mile away.

Not content with a single system of front, support and reserve trenches, Falkenhayn was well ahead by spring with a second system to the rear of the forward works.

Opposite Medical aid during gas attack. Picture by A. O. Spare.

So far as Joffre and French were informed, they were undismayed, optimistic still of early victory. Joffre's plan, to strike converging blows from Champagne and Artois on the bulging enemy salient in northern France, driving deep behind the German lines, appealed to French, but London was dubious. Apprehensively, the War Council awaited the offensive as something of a test case. If a major advance proved impossible on that front, the argument for re-deploying British resources elsewhere might be taken up.

Britain's contribution to the offensive was to be in the Artois   49 venture, planned for March as a combined Anglo-French attack. There were disruptions from the start. Joffre insisted he could not go ahead unless the British relieved French troops holding an allied salient around Ypres; Sir John French claimed he had not got the men to spare. Reinforcements for the BEF arrived slowly, some diverted to the Dardanelles. The new arrivals – including several regular divisions assembled from foreign garrisons, the Indian Corps, and the 1st Canadian Division – brought the British strength

General Erich von Falkenhayn, Moltke's successor.

up to thirteen divisions, excluding cavalry. It now provided two armies.

But the extra forces had been used to extend the British front, not to create reserves.

Aggravated by Joffre's obduracy and stung by mounting French criticism that the British were not 'pulling their weight', the commander of the BEF resolved to attack without his allies. On 10 March, while a thirty-five minute artillery bombardment hammered the German line, four divisions of the 1st Army (the Lahore, the Meerut, the 7th and the 8th) prepared to leave the trenches and advance on a two mile front at Neuve Chapelle, between Artois itself and Ypres.

Their task was not enviable. Since the start of the trench war, every soldier had learned to keep his head down. It was the cardinal rule for survival. Now he was asked not only to raise his head but to heave his whole body out of the protecting trench and make for the enemy. Nor was he offered the hope of a sudden sprint. Had the ground been kind and the distance short enough, he was still obliged to hump a daunting load.

British troops had arrived in France burdened with every item of equipment, useful and superfluous, which could be hung upon them. Much had quickly been left at the roadside. Still, the infantryman went into action with a personal load of half a hundredweight.

His mobility was further hazarded by barbed wire, hopefully destroyed by shell fire, but more likely churned up and concealed in the soft earth. 'Barbed wire terrified and obsessed the infantryman,' declared an officer. 'All his daring and courage came to naught when he ran against an incompletely destroyed network. He knew he would get caught and lacerated in its entangled mass.' And he knew the machine guns would do the rest.

Again, on the narrow front appointed at Neuve Chapelle, the entire advance could be enfiladed by flanking German field artillery. French's gesture of independence was a hopeless one.

Hours after the time set for the assault, the British generals learned that their troops had failed to break through the German front line. Disastrously, an order went out to press the attack 'regardless of loss'. When it was at last called off due to lack of ammunition the advance was no further forward and the attackers had lost more than 13,500 men. Three weeks later, an assault by the French 1st and 3rd Armies in the Champagne theatre failed at enormous cost.

Neither Joffre nor French was deterred from going forward. German losses had been heavy too, it was pointed out. Shortage of munitions, the narrowness of the attack sectors, and the inability of the allies to synchronize were propounded as contributory, but henceforward avoidable, factors in the repulse.

Joffre now proposed a bigger, better organized offensive for the end of April. 'Such a blow on the enemy,' he told French, 'that the greatest results may follow and our movement become an important step to final victory.' French reaffirmed his desire to co-operate.

In fact, the Germans struck first, with unlooked for ingenuity.

On 22 April, the Ypres salient, then about ten miles at the base and projecting five miles into German-occupied territory, was held by the British 2nd Army, including Canadians, with French Algerian and Territorial troops on the left. Facing them was the German 4th Army. Throughout the morning there had been heavy shelling of Ypres and its approaches, but this eased in the afternoon until the front was peaceful. At 5 p.m. a furious bombardment suddenly recommenced, after which a strange yellowish-green cloud appeared from the German line in the north of the salient, drifting low on the evening breeze towards the allies.

'It burned in my throat,' wrote a Frenchman who encountered it, 'caused pains in my chest and made breathing all but impossible. I spat blood and suffered dizziness. We all thought that we were lost.'

Reported Sir John French: 'What followed is practically indescribable. The effect of the gas was so overwhelming that the whole of the positions occupied by the French divisions was rendered incapable of any resistance. It was impossible at first to realize what had actually happened. Fumes and smoke obscured everything. Hundreds of men were thrown into a stupor, and after an hour the whole position had to be abandoned together with fifty guns.'

Horrified by the mysterious vapour, the French colonial troops in its immediate path had streamed from the front, followed by the French Territorials. The German infantry, plodding in the wake of the drifting cloud, was able to advance through a gap of four miles without opposition. Outflanked, the Canadians abutting the French lines struggled to seal the breach. Thanks to a failure of some of the gas cylinders, the Canadians and the adjacent British had escaped contamination. They fought doggedly.

A week later, when the battle subsided, Ypres was still within the allied line, but the salient had been much reduced. Both sides took

stock of the most sensational weapon of the war to date.

Not the least remarkable feature of the episode was that the allies had been unprepared for it. Warnings had abounded. For one thing, the Germans had already used gas against the Russians. For another, German soldiers captured in recent weeks on the Western Front had revealed that a gas attack was in preparation. At least one prisoner had carried a gas mask. As if that were not enough, British patrols had actually seen the gas cylinders in position by the salient.

'We found gas cylinders in dozens,' attested a sergeant of the Leicester Regiment involved in a raiding expedition at the end of March. 'The information was passed to headquarters.'

That such indications went unheeded evidenced both the feeble cohesion of allied intelligence and a general feeling in military circles that gas was not a practicable weapon. Ypres certainly demonstrated some drawbacks. For weeks, the Germans had postponed attacking for want of a favourable wind. Orders had been for a dawn discharge of the cylinders, but impatience and a fortuitous breeze had finally conspired to produce an evening operation, leaving the attacking infantry too little time to make ground before nightfall.

It was also true that the advancing Germans were held back by their own gas.

All the same, had the German generals been less sceptical of the new weapon, they could have exploited it more sweepingly. Expecting little from the gas, they had found themselves with a gaping breach in the allied line and insufficient reserves at hand to effect the major breakthrough that was suddenly possible. In the ensuing battle further discharges were made against the British and Canadians, who suffered heavily, but the surprise had gone and there was no panic.

Troops improvised masks from handkerchiefs damped with a solution of bicarbonate of soda, or made tie-on respirators from lint and tape. The smoke helmet, a bag covering the entire head, with goggle apertures for vision, appeared in June. Later, an effective box respirator became standard issue.

Meanwhile, French urgently telegraphed the War Office for protective apparatus, urging the earliest possible provision for retaliation in the same medium. Kitchener reminded him that the use of asphyxiating gases was contrary to the rules and usages of war as set out in the Hague Convention of 1907 (true in spirit, though the actual wording referred to gas shells, not cloud gas), but
promised to look into it.

'Before we fall to the level of the degraded Germans, I must submit the matter to the government.'

At that moment, the government was approaching transition to the coalition of May, which saw Lloyd George as minister of munitions, and sanction for the British use of gas met some delay. With its announcement on 18 May, a Major C. E. Foulkes of the Royal Engineers was promoted to lieutenant-colonel and appointed 'gas adviser' to the BEF. Foulkes had no experience with chemical warfare, but he was a resourceful officer and was soon consulting British scientists.

French was anxious that gas bombs should be dropped from aeroplanes, but the British air command declined to handle gas (as did the German air force), and its delivery remained an army responsibility. The priority of the gas service, recruited largely from university students and graduates, was to 'organize a gas attack on a large scale at the earliest possible moment' with sufficient secrecy to surprise the Germans. The method was envisaged principally as chlorine diffusion from ground cylinders on a front of several miles. It would be followed by enough troops, French told the War Office, 'to ensure a considerable tactical success'.

Interrupted by Ypres, Joffre now renewed his own offensive. The main advance, directed by his northern commander, Foch, commenced in May between Lens and Arras. It was repulsed with grim losses. At the same time, the British 1st Army made a smaller assault to Foch's left, along the valley of the Lys river towards a feature known as Aubers Ridge. The effectiveness of preliminary

Men of the 2nd Lancs Regiment, with wounded, shelter inside a British mine crater during the fighting at Aubers Ridge, 1915.

55

bombardment was curtailed by a shortage of shells, plus the deficient quality of many used.

When nine divisions of the 1st, 4th and Indian Corps attacked at dawn on 9 May, the machine-gun fire which met them was murderous. More than 11,600 troops were killed or wounded before the action was broken off at 6 p.m.

Urged by Joffre and Foch, French renewed the British offensive at nearby Festubert on 15 May. This time, a heavy bombardment had been directed at a three mile section of the German line held by a single division, though promptly reinforced by two more. For almost two weeks, a series of attacks was pressed across flat, rain-drenched country at the German entrenchments, first by regular British and Indian divisions, then by Territorials newly arrived in France and the Canadians who had fought at Ypres. The final result was a gain of about twelve hundred yards on a short front, against nearly seventeen thousand men lost. German casualties were significantly lighter.

The allied spring offensives left little doubt in many minds that new policies were needed. The French had suffered more than 102,500 casualties in twenty-four days when they called a halt to attacks in June. The British army had lost 59,275 men in a month on the Ypres salient, not to mention its other actions. As Churchill pointed out to the war cabinet, the net gain had been about eight square miles of territory, and even that was of small strategic value.

On 19 June, an overdue inquiry began into the causes of allied failures, and the material requirements of armies engaged in trench war. Held at Boulogne between the British and French munitions ministers, attended by staff officers of both nations, the conference reached some pointed conclusions.

Among other things, it was considered essential that the allies increase the ratio of their heavy guns to their field guns (the Germans had one heavy gun to two field guns; the French one to four; the British one to twenty). At least, the German ratio should be matched. There should also be, it was propounded, an allowance of one thousand rounds of ammunition for every heavy gun supporting an attack; two thousand rounds for each field gun.

The British expressed the view that a successful attack against German trenches called for a minimum thirty-six divisions and 1,150 heavy guns on a twenty-five mile front. Since the earliest Britain could provide guns, ammunition and new army units on this scale was spring 1916, her representatives felt it prudent to postpone any major offensive action in the trench war for the rest of 1915.

Joffre staunchly opposed such a pólicy.

France, he insisted, was depressed by Britain's hesitancy. In fact, France, not excluding many troops and officers, was depressed by his own failures and losses. But Joffre was buoyant and plausible. On 5 July, Kitchener, accompanying Asquith to France for talks with the French government, met its masterful general and was persuaded that the morale of his compatriots depended on a continued effort to recover the lost territories without delay. Characteristically, Joffre then won his own government by presenting his ambitions as Kitchener's.

French, for his part, still backed Joffre's original offensive plan, hoping to be ready for a new push in late August. In the interim, a British 3rd Army, made possible by reinforcements to the BEF, relieved French troops astride the Somme, and the Germans pressed ahead with their defences.

By the end of July Falkenhayn could boast an almost complete second system of trenches some two or more miles behind the first line. At this distance, it was immune to shelling by field guns unless the enemy captured the first line, by which time the Germans reasonably supposed they should have time to improvise a third line in any sector so hard pressed as to warrant it.

German heavy mortar being prepared for action.

As the weeks passed, French, susceptible to swift changes in his moods, grew less confident. On 28 July he felt 'practically certain we should not get beyond our present positions until next spring'. He disliked the area appointed by Joffre for the British attack – a flat, featureless position north of the town of Lens – and his objection became an issue of such contention that the two governments became involved.

In London it seemed a poor time to be bickering. Hope of victory in the Dardanelles was waning. Early August saw the Germans occupy Warsaw. If things got much worse for Russia her rulers might be forced into unilateral peace to avoid a popular revolution. Whatever the drawbacks, Kitchener concluded, a renewed western offensive to relieve pressure on the eastern front was imperative. France must not be upset. Joffre must be humoured.

The British army, Kitchener told French, would have to co-operate unreservedly with its allies, even if it meant 'very heavy losses indeed'. Joffre had his own way.

'The initial operations,' he instructed, 'will be carried out by thirty-five divisions in Champagne, and thirty divisions, twelve of them British, in Artois. In addition, twelve Belgian and French divisions will be ready to take part. Three-quarters of the French forces will engage in the general battle. They will be supported by two thousand heavy and three thousand field guns. ... All the chances of success are present.'

So much so, it seemed, that detailed arrangements were made to rush French and British cavalry through such breaches as were opened, and even to pursue the enemy with infantry in motor buses. The focus of the British attack was Loos, a small coal-mining town between Lens and, to its north, La Bassée. The ground was unfavourable, and the BEF had only nineteen guns per mile in support (half as many as the French).

But there was a new hope for the infantry. Foulkes's men had been working hard. They were ready to turn gas on the German line.

Zero hour for the assault at Loos was 6.30 a.m. 25 September.

Sir Douglas Haig, the general commanding the attacking 1st Army, was a reserved Scot of substantial wealth with high connections (he was a personal friend in turn of King Edward VII and King George V) and a marked vein of piety. 'We shall win,' he informed a subordinate before the battle, quoting the scripture,

'"Not by might nor by power, but by *My Spirit,* saith the Lord of Hosts".'

Gas, he hoped, would prove a telling factor, though the risks were not lost on him. Foulkes's special companies, about fourteen hundred men, had moved into the British line on the evening of the 24th to take charge of more than four hundred gas emplacements. Given a favourable wind, they would discharge chlorine gas and smoke intermittently for forty minutes before the assault. Without that wind, support would again reside in too few guns with too little ammunition.

Reports through the night suggested that morning conditions would be suitable, and at 3 a.m., when the final decision had to be made, Haig ordered the emission to proceed at 5.50 a.m. Soon afterwards, the outlook deteriorated. There was very little breeze. Anxiously, Haig contacted his corps commanders to see if the attack could be delayed. He was told it was too late to cancel orders.

At the appointed hour, amid a flurry from the British artillery, the gas release started. Problems were manifold. It was the first British operation of its kind and the gas crews contended with defective pipes, leaky joints and the hazards of German counter shelling. In some of the bays, tons of earth, thrown up by bursting shells, buried cylinders and personnel entirely; elsewhere, connections were severed and containers burst. Where leakages were heavy, the Vermorel sprayers provided for emergency decontamination proved useless.

Robert Graves, present with the Welsh Regiment, described the confusion in the crowded trenches:

'There were cries and counter-cries: "Come on!" "Get back, you bastards!" "Gas turning on us!" "Keep your heads, men!" "Back like hell, boys!" "Whose orders?" "What's happening?" "Gas!" "Back!" "Come on !" … We were alternately putting on and taking off our gas helmets and that made things worse.'

In most sectors where the wind was dangerous, gas officers stopped the discharge at their discretion. On the left, however, some received orders from divisional headquarters to continue discharging, against their better judgement, and the gas drifted across the front of the trenches.

Nevertheless, much gas was released effectively. Clambering to the top of a wooden observation post at battle headquarters, a château near the line, the sturdy, moustachioed Haig watched a great cloud of gas and smoke rolling across the flat land towards the enemy – like 'a vast prairie conflagration', reported Foulkes.

At 6.30 a.m., six infantry divisions emerged from the British

Stretcher bearers in
captured trench.
Painting by Gilbert
Rogers.

trenches. Three, the 1st, 2nd and 7th, were regulars; one, the 47th, comprised London Territorials; the other two, the 9th and 15th, were Scottish divisions of the New Army. Slowly, they advanced in khaki waves, the lines about a hundred yards apart, the troops in them a few paces from each other. The scene, as the Germans blazed through the deadly murk, is conveyed in the recollections of individual soldiers.

> The air was vicious with bullets. ... Ahead the clouds of smoke, sluggish low-lying fog, and fumes of bursting shells, thick in volume, receded towards the German trenches. ... A slight rain was falling. ...
>
> He blew his whistle and the company charged. They were stopped by machine gun fire before they had passed our own entanglements. ... The gas cylinders were still whistling and the trench full of dying men....
>
> Samson was lying wounded about twenty yards away from the front trench. Several attempts were made to get him in. ... Finally his own orderly managed to crawl out to him. Samson ordered him back, saying that he was riddled and not worth rescuing. ...
>
> A little distance from me three men hurried forward, and two of them carried a box of rifle ammunition. One fell flat to earth; his two mates halted for a moment, looked at the stricken boy and seemed to puzzle at something. Then they caught hold of the box hangars and rushed forward. The man on the ground raised himself on his elbow and looked after his mates, then sank down again on the wet ground. ...
>
> Another soldier came crawling towards us on his belly, for all the world like a gigantic lobster ... blood welled through his muddy khaki trousers. ...
>
> The sergeant seemed to be kneeling in prayer. ... In front the cloud cleared away and the black crucifix standing over the graves of Loos became revealed. 'Advance, boys!' said the sergeant. ...

In parts of the German line, the gas killed or incapacitated many defenders. A German corporal captured in a badly affected sector asserted that few of his comrades had respirators, and the weaker men were rapidly overcome. 'The stronger ones stuffed socks in their mouths, and the married decided to go to a place where there was no gas.' A captured officer declared that as soon as the gas entered his trench he lost control over his men, though they belonged to a good battalion.

The British Territorials, attacking such a sector, were luckier than most. 'Our assault, coming up behind the thick curtain of gas and smoke, practically took the enemy by surprise,' reported the divisional commander. Elsewhere, conditions were terrible. On the left, the British attack, impeded by the wayward drift of the gas there, made little progress. The 2nd Division of regulars returned choking to its own trenches.

Where the front was clear of smoke, the German fire was accurate.

Unlike the defending riflemen, whose respirators, when they had them, were simply gauze masks, the German machine-gunners wore oxygen apparatus. Their contribution was lethal. British units, disorientated by the mayhem and swirling fumes, cast about confusedly. Young and inexperienced troops in particular lost all sense of direction on the bare, bullet-swept terrain, where an occasional shed or slag heap looked much like another.

By nightfall 15,470 men, a sixth of the attacking force, were dead or wounded. Part of the German front line was in British hands, and some of Haig's troops were further forward, but reserves were desperately needed. Haig later blamed French for not producing them speedily. Road control in the rear was poorly organized, and fresh divisions were slow in moving up. Those in the concentration area, unblooded New Army units (21st and 24th Divisions) which had never seen the front lines, had already made three arduous night marches, and required yet another to reach the battlefield.

It was almost midday on the 26th before they were sufficiently refreshed to attack, by which time the Germans had brought twenty-two more battalions into their defences. The raw British troops went forward bravely, but the task was hopeless. A subsidiary attack north of Loos had failed to draw off the German reserves, and the French were getting nowhere. The 21st Division was quickly in confusion. By a heroic effort, the unseasoned 24th actually reached the enemy's second line before it was forced back.

In Champagne, as well as Artois, the French had failed dismally, but Joffre did not give up. For another month the allied offensive was pursued intermittently and expensively, without more success.

On 27 September, the British attempted to seize a dominating slag heap at Loos known colloquially as 'the dump', depending on Grenadiers to clear the enemy dug-outs in advance of the bayonet men. An officer of the 12th Royal Fusiliers described an episode in the action:

'Over the edge they found the machine-guns playing breast high and felt the sing of bullets about their ears. Men flung up their arms and toppled backwards like stormers in an old print. ... "Where are those bombers? Bloody hell! Where are those bombers?" It was the sergeant-major. There was a catch in his voice as he realized that his bombers had been caught by the machine-guns; that the attack was doomed to failure.'

On 11 October, four corps of the French 10th Army attacked in Artois, but only one of them 'gained a little ground'. Two days later, four British divisions, two of them non-regular, made the last substantial attack at Loos. The artillery bombardment made little impact on the deep German dug-outs; hand grenades were too

63

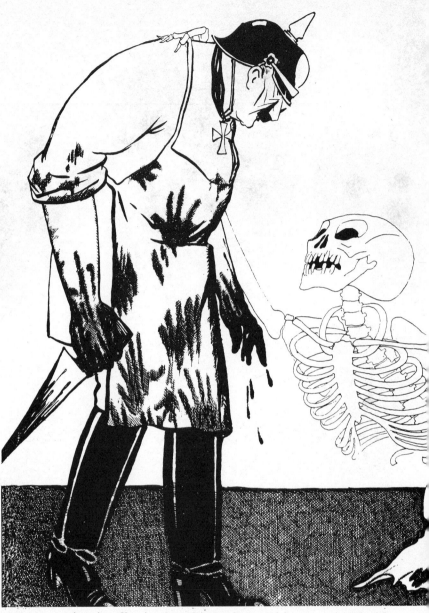

scarce to maintain effective bombing; the machine guns inevitably
claimed their toll.

'I met the bayonet men who were supposed to follow the bombers,
edging back,' wrote a witness. 'They were mostly recruits, and were
leaderless and much shaken. They cried out that the officer was
killed near the barricade. ... I went to find the other subaltern. I
found him sick and shaken by his first action, sitting as though
paralysed.'

'Remplace-moi, je suis fatiguée' by Iribe (from *La Baïonette* Vol 4, 1916).

That day, a single British division received nearly 3,800 casualties, mostly in the first ten minutes of fighting. To all intents, the Loos offensive was over. From 25 September to mid-October, in their main and supporting actions, the British had lost 61,280 soldiers, and nowhere had the German defences been broken through. In a moment of depression, French told Haig dismally that if peace were not concluded without delay England would be ruined.

'He seemed tired of the war,' Haig wrote critically.

Chapter 4

Undercurrents

One development of trench warfare for which Britain seemed particularly well equipped, yet had started a poor second to Germany, was mining: the technique of tunnelling beneath No Man's Land to place explosive charges under the enemy's defences. Few people knew more about commercial tunnelling than the British, whose tough, resourceful underground workers ranked among the world's best. Yet the army had displayed little interest. Sapper training included a meagre three days' elementary instruction in the process.

Germany's military engineers were more thorough than the British. From the onset of the trench war, they had begun to work underground.

On 20 December 1914, ten German mines were exploded on a front of about half a mile beneath the British trenches near Festubert. The victims, Indian troops of the Sirhind Brigade, already numbed by the winter and pounded by artillery, were appalled as the ground erupted, hurling earth, men, wire and sandbags skywards with terrific force. While the shocked Indians staggered dazedly to the rear, waiting German infantry pounced on the devastated positions.

Word of the new menace hit morale badly. Shells, mortar bombs, grenades and snipers were bad enough; the knowledge that not even the earth itself was neutral added a singularly unwelcome dimension to the fears of the trench men. Horrified that the enemy might be burrowing underfoot, British troops went to frantic lengths in their attempts to detect miners.

Men knelt in the squelching mud trying to discern vibrations by holding one end of a stick in their teeth, bedding the other end in the ground. Oil drums filled with water were sunk into the bottom of trenches, where shivering soldiers lay in the filth to dip their ears into the freezing liquid. A few units grew so jittery they had to be withdrawn from the line.

Opposite Miners at work in underground chamber.

Regardless of tactical potential, mining had established itself as a psychological factor the British army could no longer overlook.

In February 1915, after more German underground explosions, Kitchener authorized the formation of a special mining unit. Since the Royal Engineers had neither the required experience nor the men to spare, the service was to be manned by skilled volunteers attracted from industry. Kitchener assigned its organization to a flamboyant commercial adventurer, John Norton Griffiths, MP, known for his old school loyalist attitudes as 'Empire Jack'.

Norton Griffiths knew little about mining, but he was a tireless

67

hustler, and his business interests included a drainage contract with Manchester Corporation, employing professional tunnel diggers accustomed to working in soggy clay. These men, aptly known as 'Moles' in the excavation trade, were to provide the nucleus for the army's new service. They were quickly joined, thanks to the enthusiastic cajolery and promises of Norton Griffiths, by underground workers from all over Britain.

Officers at the RE depot where the miners were inducted had never seen such recruits. Though none admitted to being over thirty-five, their ages ranged through middle age to the sixties. Some were toothless; others white-haired. Their resilience, however, was not in doubt.

Nor, to the army's perturbation, was their stubborn independence.

Perhaps due to the unconventional recruiting methods of Empire Jack, the expectations of the miners often verged on the laughable. Granted the handsome pay, by army standards, of six shillings a day (provided they were fully skilled), some considered themselves further entitled to retain civilian rights while wearing uniform, and even to be driven to and from work by motor car. Attempts to turn them into conventional soldiers brought protests. One company, paraded for the first time, sent a delegation to inform the commanding officer that 'drill or any form of military training was not in their "contract".'

In France, service chiefs were chary. The prospect of accommodating substantial numbers of improperly disciplined, free-thinking miners in their units did not appeal to them. Indeed, French initially rejected the whole idea. But the need to respond to the increasing German use of mines converted him, and the generals soon perceived that the newcomers, if eccentric soldiers, were less than revolutionaries.

Like infantrymen, miners spent alternating periods of several days in the front line and in the rear. While at the front they worked in eight hour shifts, labouring in pairs in the narrow tunnels by candle light.

One man attacked the mud face with grafting tools, passing the waste to his mate, who crammed it into sandbags. The bags were then dragged out on ropes by the men at the tunnel mouth. Some tunnels were large enough to allow small trolleys to operate. It was arduous, dangerous work, especially in wet clay which oozed between the timbers inserted to prevent collapse.

Inured to the normal risks of their trade, the miners found a whole range of new problems at the battle front. The equipment provided from army stores was primitive. Hand-cranked ventilation blowers dated from the Crimean War. When one company asked for modern breathing equipment, it was sent a couple of underwater diving bells, as useless as they were incongruous. Disgustedly, the men improvised a system with bellows blowing into hosepipe, but there was so little oxygen at times in the tunnels that

Map 3 Trench Mining System.

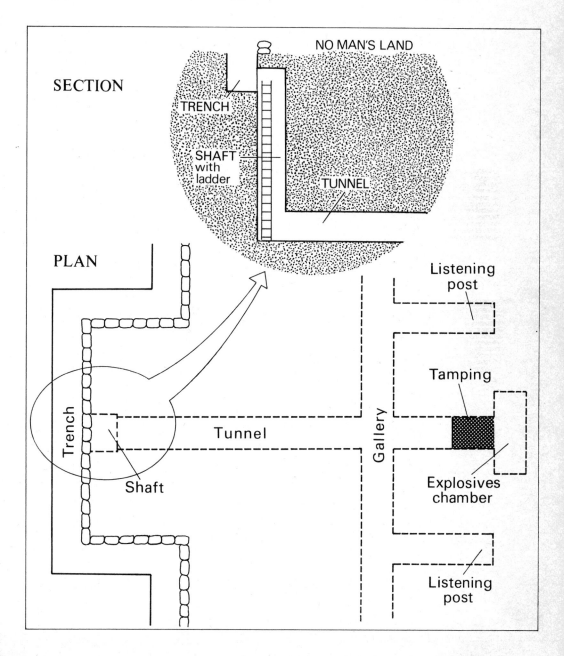

the candles would not burn. Many miners collapsed, or suffered severe headaches.

Another drawback was the need to work in silence. If the enemy detected the noise of digging, he would explode a charge in the area to shake the tunnels down, probably burying the occupants. It was safer, where possible, to use bare hands rather than risk the chink of digging tools. For this reason among others the chalk prevalent on some sectors was a qualified blessing.

Chalk was cleaner and more stable to work than clay, but it transmitted sound more readily and tended to harbour carbon monoxide given off by old explosions. It also presented disposal problems, for the white waste was a give-away to enemy aircraft.

As mining activity increased, the likelihood of simultaneous British and German digging became real on some sectors. Periodically, the British teams would press their ears to the tunnel walls, listening for the muffled noises which meant that they were not alone underground. If the Germans were indeed mining nearby, a race developed to complete work and detonate ahead of the enemy. There was no second prize, for the first explosion would destroy all chambers, and anyone caught in them.

Occasionally, tunnels from the opposing lines actually met beneath No Man's Land, giving rise to eerie subterranean battles. A subaltern named Richard Brisco became something of a mining legend after twice penetrating German tunnels in the St Eloi sector, near Ypres, and driving off enemy miners with pistol fire.

Altogether, the claustrophobic discomforts of tunnelling, added to the normal hazards of trench life, made the miner's lot an unenvied one, and the average soldier did not grudge the army's Moles their extra pay.

One of the first successful British mining ventures was at Hill 60, a notorious height on the southern shoulder of the Ypres salient. The feature was formed of earth removed from a cutting in the so-called Messines Ridge to allow passage of the railway from Ypres to the border town of Comines. Its commanding view of the front made its occupation desirable to both sides, and it was contested savagely.

When the BEF took over the sector from the French, Hill 60 was in enemy hands, and so deeply fortified that artillery made little impression on the defence. Undermining seemed the best prelude to an assault. Work began on 8 March from the forward British trenches, three main tunnels being driven towards the German

earthworks. Conditions were atrocious. Mud squirted and squelched in the initial shafts, and the decomposing bodies of men killed earlier had to be dug out and smothered in quicklime.

By 16 March, it had become unpleasantly apparent from noises detected in the tunnels that the Germans were digging too. From now on the British miners clawed unsparingly in their dark, clammy burrows, inching forward at an agonizing twelve or so feet a day.

One British tunnel ran into a German gallery. As the miners crouched silently in the darkness, a gunshot reverberated stunningly in the chamber, sending them scrambling back to the entry shaft. 71

Later they returned cautiously with a small charge and blew in the German tunnel.

A month after digging had begun the tunnels were complete, up to one hundred yards in length, and the guncotton charges were dragged to the extremities. As the detonators were fixed and checked, the Germans could clearly be heard moving overhead. The mines were fired on 17 April. They flung mud, trench timbers, weapons and torn bodies nearly three hundred feet into the air, ripping huge craters in Hill 60. Immediately, infantry of the 13th Brigade climbed from the British trenches and stormed the height successfully.

The British tunnellers had shown themselves a force with which to be reckoned.

The largest single mine at Hill 60 had contained 2,700 lb of explosive. On 15 July, the British detonated the first of their really big mines, about 5,000 lb, at Hooge, a few miles north on the salient. So great was its force, reported one officer, that large trees were hurled skywards 'like matchsticks'. The debris not only buried scores of Germans in their redoubts, but killed at least ten British infantrymen waiting to attack from their own trenches.

Attacking mined positions was a job the trench soldier came to view dubiously. Though resistance was minimized by the explosive shock, consolidating an objective reduced to a gaping crater was difficult. Without enemy trenches and dug-outs for shelter, the assault troops could only crouch in the torn earth and wait for the inevitable counter-attack.

Commanders, too, had their doubts. Much of the British mining effort was dissipated in attempts to thwart enemy miners by counter-burrowing, destroying their tunnels with small charges known as camouflets. Where the work was more positive, as at Hooge and Hill 60, it was isolated and costly. About a thousand skilled men, difficult to replace, were killed, wounded or taken sick per month in the tunnelling units. Was it worth it?

At the end of 1915, the War Office took stock. Twenty tunnelling companies existed, each with up to a thousand men and increasing quantities of expensive equipment. To justify their existence, it was decided, they must be organized strategically, not merely tactically as hitherto. In consequence, the old leadership, colourful but amateurish, was superseded by the army's first Inspector of Mines, Brigadier Robert Napier Harvey, Royal Engineers.

The tunnellers had become part of the military establishment.

Throughout 1915, almost every event on the Western Front pointed out the need for fresh methods, greater efficiency in the war directorates of the embattled nations; especially Britain, whose martial system had received a severe shock. In sixteen months of fighting her regular army had virtually disappeared. By the year's end, thirty-six British divisions were on the continent, but increasingly

Explosion of British mine under German redoubt near Beaumont Hamel, 1916.

73

the BEF comprised unseasoned warriors of the New Army.

At home, recruitment had dropped off, though not before the indiscriminate enlistment of men from industry had badly hit munitions output. In October, the Kitchener method of recruitment was modified by Lord Derby's national register, aiming to regulate the distribution of manpower between army and industry. Though the voluntary principle lingered a few more weeks, its demise was inevitable. In January 1916, Great Britain turned at last to conscription.

There were few doubts that Britons would continue to serve loyally. Whatever their category – professionals, Territorials or Kitchener recruits – the troops had displayed exemplary stoicism and endurance through the early months.

By contrast, the conduct of the trench war had brought sparse glory to the executive. Time and again, Britain's military chiefs had shown their inadequacy, not only in dealing with modern war developments, but, by allowing French commanders to dominate

British front line trench and graves, Laventie, 1915.

their strategy, treating the British army as an extension of the French command. At home, British industry had consistently fallen short with armaments production. The munitions it did produce were unreliable.

Hand grenades, when they eventually arrived for the BEF, frequently failed to explode, or exploded prematurely, mutilating British soldiers. Shells burst in gun barrels, or flopped passively on to French and Belgian mud until the battlefield was strewn with British duds. Howitzer crews lived in such apprehension of being blown up by their own ammunition that they dubbed themselves the 'suicide clubs'.

Frustration and setbacks, provoking emotional responses from Sir John French, had led to unhelpful animosities at command level. In one incident, French had removed the commander of his 2nd Army, General Sir H. L. Smith-Dorrien, for proposing a tactical withdrawal following the German gas attack at Ypres. Feelings were not eased when General Sir Herbert Plumer of the 5th Corps,

who replaced Smith-Dorrien, was obliged to advocate the same
measure.

Lacking the confidence of Kitchener, and increasingly the victim
of poor health, French incurred mounting criticism as his offensives
failed. The battle of Loos brought dissent to a head. Haig, who had
never thought highly of the C-in-C, blamed him for mishandling
the reserves, concluding on 2 October that it was 'impossible to
discuss military problems with an unreasoning brain of his kind.
At any rate, no good result is to be expected from so doing.'

In this, the chief of staff in France, General Sir William

Robertson, concurred. Between them, Haig and Robertson persuaded King George V that French should be relieved of his command. Kitchener gave him scant support, and in early December the prime minister asked for the C-in-C's resignation. With some petulance, French departed. Haig stepped into his shoes.

It was the replacement of a cavalryman by yet another cavalryman, but the contrast in their temperaments was notable.

Where the old commander had been moody and variable, the new chief was consistent, resolute, a man unlikely to swerve in calamity or success. Though few even of his admirers claimed he possessed brilliance, Haig was generally held a sound, dependable commander. His qualities commended him in particular to those upset by French, and appeared consistent with the stubborn nature of the trench war. He was also nine years younger than his predecessor.

There were other significant changes.

At the top, the promotion of Robertson to CIGS (he was replaced by General Sir Launcelot Kiggell as CGS) reactivated a general staff in London which had so far been eclipsed by Kitchener's non-consultative methods, marking a perceptible decline in the great marshal's influence.

In the lower echelons, the trench soldier had emerged from the first season of allied offensives a considerably more reflective man. He had joined the war on a wave of patriotic ardour that had seemed to unite the whole nation. Now he doubted some aspects of that unity. Within months of the inception of trench warfare, Britons who had barely considered the inequalities of everyday Edwardian society were smarting at the palpable unevenness of the war burden.

There were, it seemed to many, two very different wars: one in, the other behind, the line. Admittedly, there was no practical reason why headquarters' staffs should not live and work in decent surroundings, but the extent to which some of them made themselves comfortable invited resentment. Visits to the rear often angered front line soldiers.

The experience of one infantry officer after a bloody battle was typical. He had been detailed to collect the unit's pay from corps headquarters, ten miles back from the battle front.

'Having got the money, we were informed by the military police that this beautiful untouched town was out of bounds for anyone not on the corps staff. We were not allowed to get even a cup of tea, although the teashops and cafés that abounded were full of staff officers and their clerks. We were all but put under arrest.'

Distinctions were emphasized by the fact that even junior staff officers then wore conspicuous red hat bands and gorgets, a custom later abolished for all below the rank of colonel. These markings, encouraging a misplaced sense of superiority and highlighting the staff officer's immaculate appearance against the muddy raiment of the line soldier, were known as 'badges of shame' in the trenches.

In this poem, 'Base Details', infantryman Siegfried Sassoon caught the bitterness:

> If I were fierce, and bald, and short of breath,
> I'd live with scarlet Majors at the Base,
> And speed glum heroes up the line to death.
> You'd see me with my puffy petulant face,
> Guzzling and gulping in the best hotel,
> Reading the Role of Honour. 'Poor young chap,'
> I'd say – 'I used to know his father well … '

More disillusioning perhaps was the seeming lack of urgency and commitment among civilians at home. Industrialists and their cohorts continued to live in luxury, to flaunt their wealth at social 'occasions', while their factories turned out dud munitions. Worse, because it was less expected, the factory workers themselves contributed to the shortage of armaments by repeated stoppages. Five million working days were lost through strikes and stoppages, mostly 'unofficial' from a trades union viewpoint, in 1915 and 1916.

Coinciding with awakening militancy over poor living stardards, war had provided the workers who remained at home with a chance to make their claims felt. Ironically, the very conditions which had nudged many men into the army were now conspiring to deprive them of supplies which could mean the difference between defeat and victory.

Factory stoppages, freely reported in the papers, bemused the trench soldier, who not only suffered filth, lice, rats, sudden violence, and all the rest for his shilling a day, but was liable to face a firing squad if he went on strike.

On the other hand, alienation from the world beyond the battle front intensified comradeship and cohesion in the line itself. Here, the trappings of social life stripped off, the basic values of character were revealed. In the trenches, the peacetime gulf between officer and private soldier was insupportable. Indeed, most regimental officers were of necessity in closer contact with their men at the front than with their fellow officers.

This novel situation – a revelation for some regular officers, who confessed to understanding their men for the first time – was consolidated by the increasing infusion of New Army personnel: men

who had never known the exaggerated distinctions between

commissioned and non-commissioned ranks that had appertained before the war.

In the professional army, the officer had tended to assume authority as a prince a crown. In the New Army, officers and other ranks had started from scratch together, made their mistakes together, found their feet together. There was little room for affectation or pretension. Respect, where it existed, had been earned on merit. And by the end of the 1915 offensives respect for regimental officers was high in the British line.

If one factor contributed to this above others it was the demonstrable readiness of young commissioned men to face the severest dangers, to lead quite literally from the front. In the fiercest weeks at Ypres, one in about twenty-nine casualties was an officer; at Neuve Chapelle, one in twenty. Such figures confirmed what every trench soldier knew from experience: that whatever his own risks, the risk to his officer was greater. It may not have been comforting, but it was more inspiring than months of hard discipline.

One result of the changing attitudes of 1915 was a tacit determination among trench units to pursue a low profile, to avoid provoking the enemy during periods between big battles. Though the generals continued to press for aggression at all times, from divisional level down sympathy mounted for preserving life and some semblance of security in the so-called quiet intervals.

As a second Christmas settled on the Western Front, the trench soldier's inclination to make the most of seasonal lulls was demonstrated by a further outbreak of fraternization in No Man's Land, despite the orders against such behaviour. At least two officers who took part were court-martialled.

On many sectors the opposed troops had a friendly understanding. In the Somme region, taken over from the French by the BEF at the end of 1915 and early 1916, 'Neither side shelled the transport and shelling never began before 8 a.m., so that we could all have breakfast comfortably before settling down to the day's work.' More than a year of sharing the misery and dangers of the front with his German counterpart had persuaded the British soldier, despite lurid propaganda put out by the government, that 'Jerry' or 'Fritz' was no monster, but just another honest soldier doing his duty.

'When a battle was on, it was kill or be killed; otherwise, the lads tried to live and let live,' recalled an infantry sergeant. Even so, British losses *between* battles were now running at three hundred a day.

Some German troops were regarded as easy-going, others as

RED CROSS OR IRON CROSS?

WOUNDED AND A PRISONER
OUR SOLDIER CRIES FOR WATER.

THE GERMAN "SISTER"
POURS IT ON THE GROUND BEFORE HIS EYES.

THERE IS NO WOMAN IN BRITAIN
WHO WOULD DO IT.

THERE IS NO WOMAN IN BRITAIN
WHO WILL FORGET IT.

THE DANGERFIELD PRINTING CO. LTD, LONDON.

hard types. Saxon regiments fell in the first category; Prussians in the latter. Silesians and Bavarians reputedly disliked too much trouble. Where the trenches were close, the Germans would occasionally intimate their desire for a quiet time by raising placards or shouting across the gap. A British officer once heard some Bavarians shouting, 'Hold your fire. The Prussians will be here next week!'

On the whole, the German trench soldier seems to have preferred facing the British – 'calm and phlegmatic' as they were character-ized – to the French, whose fiercer passions perhaps derived from fighting on their own soil. At all events the French were more feared by the enemy.

For their own part the war lords were planning other than goodwill at Christmastide.

In a memorandum to the Kaiser, Falkenhayn then alluded to Britain as the 'arch-enemy' who was cunningly using the French, Russian and Italian armies as 'her real weapons'. Russia, he con-sidered, was already paralysed; Italy's military capacity unlikely to have much effect. 'France has almost arrived at the end of her military effort. If her people can be made to see that clearly ... breaking point would be reached and England's best sword smashed from her hand.'

To this end, Falkenhayn proposed a new form of offensive by methodical stages. Each stage would be limited in territorial ob-jectives, but aimed at drawing masses of defenders on to his artillery killing grounds, where destruction would be immense. The Western Front, he had no doubt, was the key theatre for 1916.

The British staff agreed with him. In conference at Chantilly at the end of the old year, military leaders of France, Britain, Belgium and Italy, with representatives of Russia and Japan, made their first serious attempt to reach strategic unity. In view of the principle they agreed – namely, for a simultaneous general offensive in 1916 – Robertson recommended to the war committee that 'every possible division' should be sent to the Western Front; commitments elsewhere pared to a minimum.

Opposite 'Red Cross or Iron Cross?' – Anti-German war poster.

Withdrawal from the Dardanelles, already in progress, lent force to this, and the committee agreed with him. Even Kitchener, absent from Chantilly and previously doubtful of the possibilities for advance, thought that 'a violent offensive' in the coming season might persuade the Germans to ask for terms.

As the second winter of the trenches reached its depths, a conflict was stirring in the minds of Europe's war chiefs that would make the battles of 1915 look like skirmishes.

Chapter 5

The Somme (I)

Soon after Christmas, Joffre and Haig began planning their 1916 offensive on the Western Front. Ideas differed. Haig, dreaming of dominating the northern flank, wished to attack in Flanders. Joffre opted for the Somme region (by early 1916, the British line ran from the Somme to beyond Ypres) where the allies could advance side by side. The French commander favoured preparatory attacks in spring to 'wear down' the German forces before the main action in summer. Haig preferred to husband allied resources for the big attack, dispensing with preliminary offensives.

They settled for a compromise in which Haig's view prevailed on the timing, Joffre's on the location. The operation would be launched on 1 July as a combined French and British assault on a sixty mile front athwart the Somme from Lassigny to Arras.

Meanwhile, in February, allied planning was cut short by Falkenhayn, who once more struck the first major blow of a violent year. In pursuance of his policy of bleeding France to death by compelling her leaders to 'throw every man they have' into the defence of some special feature of the battle front, Falkenhayn aimed his hammer at Verdun, a dated but emotive stronghold guarding the historic pass by the Meuse valley. The old forts at Verdun were neglected, and the French trenches forming a salient round them were in poor repair. Communications with Verdun were precarious.

It was, as Falkenhayn perceived, a death trap to which the French would cling at first with sentimental fervour, then, as the battle built up, convinced that the very fate of their country hinged on its defence.

The German attack, commanded by the Kaiser's son, Crown Prince William, began on 21 February with a bombardment of such intensity that the wooded and arable countryside of the Meuse was churned into an eerie brown 'moonscape'. Darkly the massed legions of the Crown Prince loomed across the ravaged land. Predictably, the French garrison received orders to stand firm while Joffre spurred reserves to Verdun from his other fronts.

Opposite Battle-ravaged wood, the Somme.

General Henri Pétain of the French 2nd Army hastened to take charge of the resistance, and diversionary measures were urged on France's allies.

In Russia offensive operations were pushed forward at Lake Narocz in the hope of relieving pressure on Verdun; but the main attack in the east by General Brusilov's army was too late to assist the French. Inexorably the Germans pummelled the salient.

83

'We had never experienced its like,' recalled a French sergeant. 'Shells of all calibres kept raining on our sector. The trenches had disappeared, filled with earth. We crouched in shell holes, increasingly smothered by the mud from explosions. The air was unbreathable. Our blinded, wounded, crawling and shouting soldiers kept falling on top of us and died splashing us with their blood. It was living hell.'

The hell of Verdun, one of the bloodiest battles in French history, persisted for five months, throwing an onerous burden on the British front. The more desperately Joffre needed the planned Somme offensive to ease the pressure on Verdun, the less able he became to contribute his intended force. By May it seemed doubtful if he could spare any troops.

In June, though French divisions from the Somme were sent to the Meuse, it was probable that a small French army of six divisions, with two in reserve, would be available: eight divisions against the forty Joffre had originally intended to put into the joint attack.

That month the French premier, Aristide Briand, visited Haig at his headquarters. Briand urged that the Somme offensive should go ahead without delay. 'He wished our attack to be hastened,' wrote Haig, 'because General Pétain had stated that "the game was up. ... The French army could not go on," etc., unless the British attacked at once.' Haig could not promise to advance the date, but he was prepared to launch the offensive as a major British enterprise.

For the first time the BEF would be a senior not a junior partner. Briand left 'full of compliments for the British army and of confidence in me', as Haig put it.

The total strength of the BEF, including dominions troops, was now fifty-eight divisions, a 4th Army having been added to the existing three. The 4th Army, commanded by General Henry Rawlinson, whom Haig reckoned his best infantry commander, was to form the main body of the Somme attack, with a corps of General Allenby's 3rd Army on the left. The sixty mile offensive front originally planned for the combined assault was forgotten. Haig concentrated on eighteen miles of the front.

He felt confident of success, 'with God's help'. At a service conducted by his chaplain, a cleric of the Church of Scotland, the British commander was much impressed by a sermon on the strength of prayer in battle, illustrated by the devotions of the Scottish troops at Bannockburn. Haig arranged for the padre to be at his advanced headquarters when the attack commenced.

General Henry Rawlinson, commander of the 4th Army which was to form the main body of the Somme attack.

The trench soldier regarded the change of seasons with mixed feelings. Winter's end, bringing warmer, drier weather, meant a lot in the front line. Where shell fire had been moderate, vales and hillsides took on colour. Flora and fauna, stirring by the earthworks, brought glimpses of enchantment to the sentinels. On the other hand, such signs presaged activity of a less attractive kind. Wrote soldier poet Alan Seeger of the approaching campaign season:

> I have a rendezvous with Death
> At some disputed barricade,
> When Spring comes back with rustling shade
> And apple-blossoms fill the air –
> I have a rendezvous with Death
> When Spring brings back blue days and fair.

On the undulating chalk downlands north of the Somme river, 1916   85 remained relatively quiet into summer. The action was centred on Verdun. Falkenhayn knew the British were concentrating forces on the southern section of their front, but his commitment to the Meuse left no reserve for spoiling tactics. The German 2nd Army in the Somme department lacked the numbers to do more than stand on defence.

Along the sector of Haig's proposed offensive, from the lowlands of the Somme river itself, across the wood-strewn downs to the valley of its northern tributary, the Ancre, and on to the bosky salient round the German-held village of Gommecourt, the trenches basked in relaxing sun.

'A few rare shells disturb the mustard and darnel blossoming along the parapet. The men rest during the afternoon. At stand-to, this summer evening almost conjures one to believe that war is a pleasant state,' declared one infantryman. 'Across the valley, the air is turning pearl grey, with here and there brown smudges where Fritz cooks his evening meal.'

Behind the British line, an almost ceaseless trundling of troops and wagons indicated the massing of 400,000 men, 100,000 horses, 455 heavy guns and howitzers, and all the equipment and supplies attendant to launching nineteen divisions at the enemy. Two more stood in close support; a further eight, including five cavalry divisions, in headquarters reserve.

Since roads and villages on the sparsely populated downs were unable to contain such an army, camps had to be built in proximity to the front. Hospitals were constructed, byways improved, bridges erected, an entire communications system set out. For the first time in the trench war, the British prepared prison 'cages' for such Germans as were captured in the attack.

Novel, too, was the frequency of British aircraft in the summer sky. An original four squadrons in France had now grown to twenty-seven squadrons with about 420 machines on operational service. Increased numbers had produced dramatic changes in the deployment of aircraft, particularly the replacement of lone spotting and strafing missions by formation flying, the planned use of air bombing, and the introduction of close-escort operations.

For the first time, the Royal Flying Corps was co-operating on a substantial scale with the army's efforts. Thanks to the concentration of German aircraft against the French, the RFC was able to establish complete air control on the Somme, with 185 machines in the area. Apart from reconnaissance, reporting troop movements and spotting for artillery, they successfully bombed enemy railway centres behind the front.

Map 4 The Somme
Battleground, 1916.

In other areas of preparation, tunnels were driven for nineteen mines, including eight giant ones, which were to be exploded immediately before the assault. A large quantity of gas was also brought up but, due partly to the infantry's dislike of its storage in the trenches, partly from distrust of the unpredictable summer winds, most of the cylinders in the line were released hastily several days before the troops attacked.

Preliminary shelling of the German defences commenced on 24 June. Heavy guns, one per fifty-seven yards, were still less numerous than hoped, but substantially outnumbered those the enemy had on the sector. Artillery orders were that the bombard-   87 ment would intensify to maximum effect just prior to the assault, blanketing the front German trenches. As the infantry went in, the heavy guns would lift back to the enemy's second line while the field guns would 'creep back by short lifts' – an early reference to the creeping barrage familiar later.

The method stipulated for the assault – dense waves of walking infantry – made no concessions to the lessons of 1915. Fifteen divisions of Rawlinson's 4th Army were to mount the main attack on a front of fifteen miles north of the River Somme. To the left, three divisions of Allenby's 3rd Army would advance in the Gommecourt area. On the right, five divisions of the French 6th Army would go into action on an eight mile front, mainly south of the river.

Facing the British attack, the Germans had six divisions in the front line and four and a half in close reserve. Though their numerical inferiority was offset by formidable positions, including a string of fortified villages linked with the trenches, British commanders hoped that the combined effects of artillery bombardment, mining, and gas and air attacks, would have done much to neutralize the enemy defence system before the infantry went in.

On 30 June, the eve of the assault, Haig wrote approvingly 'The men are in splendid spirits. Several have said that they have never before been so instructed and informed of the operation before them. The wire has never been so well cut, nor the artillery preparation so thorough. I have personally seen all the corps commanders and one and all are full of confidence.'

Optimism was more evident than its origins. In some respects the British force was better supplied and equipped than in 1915, yet many more of its men were inexperienced. The 8th Corps, assigned to the left of Rawlinson's line, was packed with troops who had seen no fighting whatsoever since reaching France. Those who had seen action in the offensives of the previous year could hardly avoid the fact that the techniques which had brought disaster at Loos were still in vogue. Yet attitudes were remarkably sanguine.

To some extent, this could be explained by the changed command. The feeling that the failures of 1915 were French's fault, that things would be right now that Haig had charge, was strong in the BEF. Again, the great masses of assembled troops, and the remorseless flow of shells towards the German trenches during the week-long bombardment, built up confidence. The most cynical of old soldiers had to admit he would not have cared to be in 'Jerry's' boots.

One battalion commander assured his men that, after such a

barrage, they could advance with sloped arms, smoking their pipes, and come to no harm. The encouragement was typical. 'You won't need rifles,' a Newcastle 'pals' battalion was told jokingly. 'A rat could not have survived in the German lines.'

The sight of cavalry streaming forward enhanced expectations.

Haig's preparations were based on the assumption that the first day of the offensive would advance the British front on average rather more than two miles, level with the village of Pozières, central to the battle front. After that, the aim would be a break-through. Cavalry would then surge on to the town of Bapaume, six miles beyond Pozières, wheel north and pour into the open country in the German rear.

Three mounted divisions had been brought up for this purpose. Together with a supporting force of infantry, they were to act as an independent command under General Sir Hubert Gough, charged with exploiting the breakthrough. Haig had little doubt that if he could reopen a war of movement his generals would quickly get the upper hand.

The first assault was timed for 7.30 a.m.

In the early hours of the morning the infantry columns moved to their forward positions through a clear, moonless night, enlivened by ceaseless gun flashes. The rumble of artillery smothered the sounds of the laden men. Dawn brought a perfect day. Where the ground was suitable the troops crawled out beyond the front line and lay waiting in No Man's Land. Elsewhere they packed the trenches, fiddling with rifles and bayonets, talking or reflecting quietly amid mounting tension.

Most were outwardly calm. Some prayed. Others fingered photo-graphs of their families or belatedly scrawled their last wills in their paybooks.

Men who were present later recalled a few young soldiers weeping and the odd case of hysteria, but outbreaks of joking and laughing were more prevalent, inspired variously by bravado, real confidence, or a special rum ration. One or two men were reported drunk. Some soldiers refused the liquor, preferring to keep their heads clear.

Overleaf The Somme, 1916. A soldier keeps watch while his mates rest in the front line.

At 7.28 a.m., the main salvo of mines went up with a roar which drowned even the bursting of heavy shells. Two of the big mines contained twenty-four tons of explosive each. Earth blotted the sky to hundreds of feet, hurling a patrolling aircraft violently sideways.

As the noise and debris subsided, a curious silence pervaded the countryside. The British barrage had ceased while the gunners

realigned on their deeper targets. The sun was shining. Men were conscious of bird song. Suddenly whistles and shouts began to ring along the line and, for as far as the eye could see, dusty figures rose from the ground, hefted rifles across their chests, and started forward.

In some sectors, it seemed for a moment as if the opposition had indeed been knocked out. 'For some reason,' recollected a Bradford private, 'nothing happened to us at first. We strolled along as if walking in a park.' A hare got up and sprinted through the summer grass. With schoolboy bravura, some units got under way by kicking footballs towards the German lines. Officers waved their troops on with swagger canes. Bagpipes skirled from Scottish battalions.

The notion of enemy impotence was fleeting.

In the German positions, the British bombardment had proved more spectacular than crippling. Shells and mines had destroyed substantial sections of the trenches, but the troops themselves had sat out the barrage in deep, blast-proof dug-outs, aware that the expected assault could not commence until the shelling lifted. Immediately this happened, they had clambered up the steep shafts to the surface with their rifles and machine guns, running to the nearest trenches or shell craters.

The following is a German officer's impression of the attack:

> As soon as we were in position, a series of extended lines of British infantry were seen moving forward from their trenches. The first line seemed to continue without end to right and left. It was quickly followed by a second line, then a third and fourth. They came on at a steady pace as if expecting to find nothing alive in our front trenches. ... A few moments later, the rattle of machine gun and rifle fire broke from our whole line.

At the same time, signals from the German front brought a carefully ranged artillery barrage on to No Man's Land. The effect on the British advance was devastating.

> Whole sections appeared to fall. All along the line, Englishmen could be seen throwing their arms into the air and collapsing, never to move again. Badly wounded rolled about in their agony, while other casualties crawled into shell holes for shelter. But the British soldier has no lack of courage. ... His lines, though badly shaken and with many gaps, now came on faster. ... The noise of battle became indescribable.

In the German trenches, the shouting of orders and shrill cheers as the British charged forward could be heard above the fusillade of small arms and the thunder of artillery.

British machine gunners in gas helmets, the Somme, 1916.

With all this were mingled the moans of the wounded, cries for help and the last screams of death. Again and again the lines of British infantry broke against the German defences like waves against a cliff, only to be beaten back. It was an amazing spectacle of unexampled gallantry.

For many British troops, hopes of a walkover had been shattered within seconds of the order to advance. Some died before they could clear their own trenches, pitching backwards on those still trying to scramble out. Others, often the leading officers and n.c.o.s, were hit after a few steps. Among them, the commander of a New Army battalion was dragged to cover by his men, who went forward without him.

A number were saved from serious head injury, as they left the trenches, by a new item of British equipment: the steel helmet. Bewildered by the unexpected and ubiquitous violence, the men moved forward automatically. 'We had no idea what it was going to be like,' said an Irish soldier. 'A few yards from the trench, a whizz bang caught my sergeant and his head disappeared.' Many 93 emotions were reported afterwards by the survivors – astonishment, fury, blind terror – but few faltered.

Swept by traversing machine guns, hindered in many places by uncut wire, the rigid, slow-moving formations were straddled by German shells. To add to the horror, a five thousand pound British mine exploded late, crippling men in several advancing battalions. Wave upon wave of infantry was shattered. Following echelons saw those ahead mown down; leading groups, clinging to desperately won positions, waited in vain for reinforcements which had, in turn, been massacred.

Throughout a day that was to set new records in man's destruction by his own kind, the slaughter continued with little gain to the attacking force. Only on the right, where the fortified villages of Montauban and Mametz were taken by the 13th and 15th Corps of Rawlinson's army, was there anything like success.

A Manchester n.c.o. whose unit won ground here, provided a glimpse of the price paid:

> Just in front of me lay a boy I had cursed the night before for being drunk. He lay quite flat, and might have been resting, except there was a big ragged hole at the base of his skull where a bullet had come out. Next to me, a man was trying with grimy hands to dab a field dressing on the back of a lance corporal who had been shot through the chest and sat up clutching his knees and rocking to and fro. My platoon officer lay on his back. His face and hands were as white as marble. His lungs were labouring like bellows. In a minute or two, he was dead. 'D'you think there's any chance for us, sergeant?' a man whispered. I said it would be all right.

In the central sectors, advances gained no footing. The fortified village of Thiepval inflicted terrible punishment. A battalion commander attacking nearby recalled catching sight of 'heaped up masses of British corpses suspended on the German wire in front of the Thiepval stronghold'. As he watched, more men advanced in 'orderly procession' to swell the weight on the entanglements.

As the attack broke down, parties of shocked and leaderless men began to drift back across the battlefront. A field officer described the fate of some of them:

> 'Where are you going?' I ask. One says one thing, one another. They are marched to the water reserve, given a drink and hunted back to fight. Another more formidable party cuts across from the south. They mean business. They are damned if they are going to stay; it's all up. A young subaltern heads them off. They push by him. He draws his revolver and threatens them. They take no notice. He fires. Down drops a British soldier at his feet. They turn back. ... It is late afternoon. ... The Germans launch an overwhelming counter-attack which proves successful.

On the left of Rawlinson's army, one division crossed the German trenches, to be forced back later; otherwise the whole assault went amiss.

Haig's reaction to failure here was bitter. In his belief, the 3rd Army's attack on the adjacent Gommecourt salient, though beaten off, provided a special opportunity for Rawlinson's 8th Corps. 'The 8th Corps (General Sir A. G. Hunter-Weston) said they began well, but as the day progressed were forced back,' wrote the C-in-C. 'I am inclined to believe from further reports that few of the 8th Corps left their trenches.'

Since the corps suffered very nearly fifteen thousand losses that day, including some of the highest of all divisional casualties, it was a strange observation.

Gradually, from the fearful confusion of the assault, casualty reports filtered through to headquarters. In many instances they defied prompt belief. Entire units had practically disappeared by evening. Thirty-two battalions had sustained more than five hundred casualties each. Four of them – three from the New Army and one from Newfoundland – had more than six hundred of their men killed or wounded, including the 10th West Yorks with an almost complete loss of 710 casualties, about sixty per cent fatal.

Final figures for the first day of the battle of the Somme revealed a staggering total loss of 57,470 men. Of these, 19,240 died, 35,493 were wounded, 2,152 were missing and 585 were prisoners.

One in every two men of the entire attacking force (143 battalions) was a casualty; three out of four in the case of officers. Such a toll of young British manhood was unprecedented in British military history. In a few hours, the BEF's losses had far exceeded Britain's battle casualties in all the years of the Crimean and Boer Wars combined.

Haig admitted no shock. On 2 July, when the yet incomplete casualty figures for the previous day already stood at more than forty thousand, and were rising, he commented 'This cannot be considered severe in view of the numbers engaged, and the length of the front attacked.' The philosophy augured the grim era of attrition which lay ahead.

German losses on 1 July were hard to estimate. Daily casualty returns were not normal in the Kaiser's army, but an outstanding historian of the Somme fighting, Martin Middlebrook, has calculated their losses at about eight thousand men, of whom 2,200 were known to be prisoners. By this reckoning, British losses outnumbered German by seven to one – oddly enough, in almost the same ratio as the British force involved outnumbered its opponents.

That the Germans defended as stubbornly, and sometimes as recklessly, as the British attacked, was evidenced by many tributes. In places, they ignored the cover afforded by their earthworks in order to train their weapons most effectively.

'The Germans were brave men, idiotically brave,' attested one British soldier. 'They actually knelt, even stood, on top of their parapet, within less than 150 yards of us.'

By the morning of 2 July, the achievements of the opening day of the offensive could be appraised. Only in the far south, had territorial gains come near to expectation. In the centre, where it had been proposed to overrun the fortified village of La Boiselle and open the main road to Bapaume for the cavalry, the heaviest sacrifices of the day had proved unavailing.

Here, two Tyneside brigades were so immolated that their dazed survivors were unfit for fighting for several months. Seven battalions had lost on average three-quarters of their manpower. For this price, a meagre twenty acres had been wrested from the enemy.

In the north, the German stronghold of Gommecourt remained intact. Indeed, of thirteen fortified villages among the day's objectives, only two were in British hands the next morning. Nowhere had the German second line been penetrated. Ironically, the best progress had been made by the small French force on the right flank, where the Germans, assuming Joffre to be preoccupied with Verdun, had somewhat neglected their defences.

In this situation, Haig resolved to concentrate on exploiting the comparative successes of his right wing. The left of Rawlinson's

Mule-drawn railway trucks for evacuating wounded in the Carnoy valley.

army, which the C-in-C deemed 'to want looking after', was placed under General Gough, whose breakthrough assignment already seemed a faded hope.

At the same time the Germans, calling a halt at Verdun, began diverting troops and guns to the Somme front. As July progressed, with small British inroads in the south at expensive cost, the campaign ceased to bear the mark of a piercing thrust and took on the nature of a grim and obdurate slogging match. By the end of the month, concern in London was making itself felt.

'The powers that be,' noted Haig, 'are beginning to get a little uneasy in regard to the situation.' The CIGS was anxious to know 'whether a loss of say 300,000 men will lead to really great results, because if not we ought to be content with something less than we are now doing'.

Haig was steadfast. On 3 August, penning his 'Principle on which we should act', he wrote unequivocally, '*Maintain our offensive*. Our losses in July's fighting totalled about 120,000 more than they would have been had we not attacked. They cannot be regarded as sufficient to justify any anxiety as to our ability to continue the offensive.'

Opposite Pack-horse loaded with trench boots.

99

Chapter 6

The Somme (II)

The frustrations of trench warfare, combined with the mounting cost of trying to overcome the deadlock, inspired a crop of mechanical and chemical inventions designed to assist the British soldier. Some appeared during the Somme fighting; others were abandoned at the testing stage.

Apart from the contributions of civilian inventors, both the War Office and the Ministry of Munitions conducted experiments on a wide range of devices and substances, from alleged battle winners to more modest appliances. Most of the ambitious proposals proved impractical, including:

A plan to scatter powdered calcium arsenide by shell fire. In dry weather, it was predicated, this would be ingested by the enemy as dust, causing arsenic poisoning. In moist weather, it was supposed to form a toxic gas, arseniuretted hydrogen. Tests, however, were disappointing, and the scheme was dropped.

A plan to fire fine coal dust over the German lines, then ignite it to cause the type of explosion experienced in mine disasters. Alternatively, volatile oil might take the place of the coal particles. As it happened, neither medium proved successful other than in a confined space.

A plan to jam the mechanism of enemy small arms and artillery by dispersing carborundum powder over the German positions. At first commended for its apparent simplicity, the project eventually raised more snags than could be handled.

One of the few really helpful innovations at the beginning of the Somme campaign involved nothing more deadly or destructive than smoke, generated in the field by red phosphorus. Smoke screens were not new, but hitherto they had been created mainly by burning 'candles'. For the first time on the Somme, the British projected smoke bombs on a substantial scale from the 4-inch Stokes mortar.

Providing a range (later improved) of 350 yards, this greatly facilitated the placing of smoke where it was wanted, and many infantry assaults were assisted.

Unfortunately, 4-inch mortars were not plentiful, nor could the special companies which operated them be everywhere. About five thousand smoke bombs were fired in forty-six operations on 1 July. Though an unprecedented effort to screen infantry movement, it was hardly consistent with the scale of the offensive, and the rate of discharge was not maintained in the ensuing week. Later in the campaign, the Stokes mortar was also employed to fire tear gas.

German machine-gun
(Maxim) on Western
Front.

A less successful, if more daunting, innovation tried out on the Somme was the flame thrower. The Germans had introduced their portable *flammenwerfer* to the Western Front in 1915. As a result, the British Ministry of Munitions produced two portable devices with short-range jets. Both were so dangerous and cumbersome that the chances of carrying them within effective distance of the enemy trenches were remote. Greater faith was placed in a heavy machine, with a range of seventy yards or more, designed for use in fixed installations.

By locating this apparatus in underground galleries ahead of the British line, it could be brought to bear on the German trenches on certain parts of the front.

Installation was a laborious process.

Apart from the preliminary mining involved, the large throwers weighed two tons apiece and required up to three hundred man-journeys to lug them into situation piece by piece. The fuel containers, filled with a mixture of light and heavy oils (propulsion was by compressed air), weighed more than two hundred pounds each.

Nevertheless, the components of four heavy machines were

hauled into subterranean chambers and assembled within sixty yards of the German front line at the end of June. One gallery was blown in by a shell and its occupants entombed before the attack began. Another shell damaged a second apparatus beyond repair. The two remaining machines were mounted ten feet and seventeen feet below the surface. To force the jets through the earth's crust, extending tubes were used, fitted at the head with steel cutters.

At zero hour on 1 July, the oil was turned on and ignited. Streams of flame, crowned with dense plumes of black smoke, leaped towards the enemy, scorching the ground for a distance of about ninety yards. The sight was terrifying, but the results were limited. Though the Germans were forced from the immediate vicinity, leaving a few charred bodies, the length of trench abandoned was too slight to be exploited effectively.

Flame throwers were abandoned by the British on the Somme before summer was out. The effort involved in bringing the large machines into action was disproportionate to any gain, while the portable machines proved a worthless encumbrance. Of five deployed in a brigade attack on 10 July, none achieved the minimal distinction of being fired.

While the Germans persisted with portable *flammenwerfers* throughout the war, despite the ease with which their crews were picked off by marksmen, British flame-thrower personnel themselves extemporized a better trench weapon from their oil drums. These were set into the ground in angled batteries, forming the barrels from which smaller drums were fired by high explosive.

Filled with oil and cotton waste, these primitive projectiles were detonated on target by time fuses, littering the enemy with burning material.

Known as the Livens projector after the officer who first thought of it, this weapon was eventually standardized and factory manufactured with a range of about a mile. Though less than accurate, its advantages were cheapness and the variety of the substances, prepared or improvised, which could be hurled from it.

Early Livens projectors, with a far shorter range, were used at the battle of Pozières Ridge on 23 July. Nine days earlier, the second great assault of the Somme had broken into the German support line southwest of Pozières, on a spine of downland running to the British right. Now, as the whirling oil drums hurtled down on some German heads, the 13th Corps of Rawlinson's army moved forward to win the crest, while the 1st Anzac Corps captured Pozières itself.

Oil projectors and other such novelties were overshadowed by the menace of gas warfare development.

THE
WIPERS TIMES.
OR
SALIENT NEWS.

No 4. Vol 2.	Monday. 20th March, 1916.	PRICE 50 CENTIMES.

HAS YOUR BOY A MECHANICAL TURN OF MIND?   YES!

—o—o—o—o—

THEN BUY HIM A

FLAMMENWERFER

INSTRUCTIVE—AMUSING.

—o—o—o—o—

Both young and old enjoy,
This natty little toy.

—o—o—o—o—

GUARANTEED ABSOLUTELY HARMLESS

—o—o—o—o—

Thousands Have Been Sold.

—o—o—o—o—

Drop a postcard to Messrs. ARMY, RESEARCH and CO., when a handsome illustrated catalogue will be sent you.

On both sides of the front troops sought ways of dispelling gas, but without much luck. Shells and bombs fired into the deadly clouds failed to destroy them, though the Germans expended a lot of ammunition in the attempt. British soldiers cleared gas from the bottom of their trenches by lighting fires. On the same principle, the French and Germans sometimes prepared long strings of fires along their parapets to lift drifting gas, a method demanding huge supplies of fuel and dry weather.

In Britain, the emotions aroused by gas warfare produced many inventive suggestions for the protection of the soldiers. One, tested early in 1916, postulated a system of oil pipes along the front trenches fitted with jets which could be ignited in a gas attack: a more sophisticated version of the string of fires. It worked well on an experimental scale, but was hardly feasible in the battleground situation.

An academic inventor urged bombing chlorine clouds with black powder to produce relatively harmless potassium sulphate fumes. Among other snags, the idea suffered the set back that chlorine was rapidly replaced by battle gases with different properties. Several suggestions involved sucking or channelling gas clouds to uninhabited dispersal areas behind the lines: for instance, by the use of giant vacuum tunnels.

More sensible, to many minds, was the notion of blowing away encroaching fumes, a proposition which gave rise to a controversial device named (after its inventor, the wife of a distinguished physicist) the Ayrton fan. This was a light, hinged apparatus on a stick handle, so constructed that it directed a one-way air current when flapped.

Tested against a controlled gas cloud in England, the Ayrton fan was proclaimed ineffective by army experts, and initially rejected by GHQ.

All the same, its influential backers persuaded the authorities to place a first order for five thousand fans. More than a hundred thousand were ultimately issued to the BEF, 'to no useful purpose whatever', according to its senior gas adviser, other than that the wooden handles made good fuel.

Against these defensive experiments, the offensive development of battle gases seemed disturbing.

Before the introduction of gas at Ypres in 1915, practical knowledge of the harmful effects of different gases was slight in Britain. Investigation brought surprises. Several gases with a reputation for being highly toxic – including prussic acid gas, nickel carbonyl and arseniuretted hydrogen – were found to be less harmful than

Opposite Front cover of the Wipers Times, an army magazine on sale to troops on the Western Front.

Overleaf Working party in crater of British mine exploded at Beaumont Hamel, November 1916. The crater measured 150 × 100 yards and was 80 feet deep.

105

supposed. The last, popularly considered lethal in the smallest quantities, caused little discomfort to a pig and two valiant officers exposed to a strong concentration in England.

On the other hand, sulphuretted hydrogen, familiar to those who had released it frivolously in schoolday escapades, proved unexpectedly toxic. An officer exposed to an experimental concentration lost consciousness almost immediately, though wearing a service gas helmet.

Mixed with a small proportion of carbon disulphide to increase its density, this gas was employed for a time by the army under the code name 'red star'. A large quantity was discharged on the eve of a Somme attack in mid-July, with some unpleasant consequences to its handlers. Several men were killed instantaneously by leaking cylinders and equipment. Others became delirious or went berserk.

One officer had to be held down to prevent his running amok, while a couple of the victims bit the men restraining them. Violent contortions were noted, followed by paralysis. Fires also broke out in the lines when army shells hit the stored gas, which was highly inflammable. Such dangers made the handling of red star precarious.

In the summer of 1915, production had been planned of a more favoured substance, phosgene. Manufactured in peacetime for use in the dyeing industry, phosgene possessed far deadlier properties than chlorine and was to become the predominant battle gas of all the Western Front belligerents. Among its other disconcerting attributes, it could be breathed in fatal doses without great discomfort (with chlorine, coughing and choking limited the intake) and had a deceptive delayed effect.

Even small intakes of phosgene were liable to cause alarming symptoms as much as twenty-four, even forty-eight hours later. Since exercise after the intake of phosgene, as of other gases, markedly increased its harmfulness, the false sense of well-being which often followed exposure was particularly treacherous. Cases constantly occurred of men feeling perfectly well for a time, then suddenly collapsing and dying.

By itself, phosgene could not be used from cylinders as its vapour pressure was insufficient to force it out. Like the liquid in a soda water syphon, it required the addition of a propelling agent, and chlorine gas was still useful for this purpose. A mixture of half phosgene, half chlorine, known as 'white star', was extensively employed on the Somme front.

Through August, desperate fighting resulted in only minor
108   British advances on the southern sector. To the north there was

almost no movement, all attempts to obliterate Thiepval failing. As frustration mounted increasing quantities of gas were released, especially on the British left where, on 30 August, the highest concentration to date was discharged against the flanking position of Monchy. White star was deployed from 1,250 cylinders.

Carried on a favourable wind, the gas took a severe toll of the German 23rd and 62nd Regiments, killing sixty men of one company seven kilometres behind the front. 'Very few men were carrying their gas masks,' admitted a prisoner from the 23rd Regiment. 'After this occurrence, more stringent orders were issued about always carrying masks in villages behind the lines.'

By the second half of 1916, respirators provided a fairly adequate protection against the gas from both sides, most gassing casualties arising from carelessness in the use of masks, or the surprise element of attacks. Warning systems incorporating gongs, bells, whistles and bugles were closely maintained, and troops learned to anticipate gas from the behaviour of pet animals in the trenches.

Captured tandem bicycle frame used by Germans to generate electricity for wireless in trenches.

109

According to one report 'Guinea-pigs are the first to scent the gas, and cats also complain quickly. Owls are greatly excited. Behind the front, fowls and ducks are said to have become restless a quarter of an hour before gas clouds approached.'

Gas casualties on the Somme, as elsewhere, were impossible to quantify. Both the Germans and the allies deliberately played down the effects of enemy gas, which, in any case, were often not evident until long after casualty statistics had been drawn up. Some men did not start to suffer seriously until the war was over. Certainly, the psychological and general nuisance value of gas was greater overall than its direct physical impact on the trench war.

'Every moment the English are letting off gas. We get no rest at all. Every moment there is an alarm,' a German soldier wrote in his diary. 'The plague is steadily getting worse,' declared another.

Constant apprehension, continuous warnings at all times of the day and night, and the discomfort and inconvenience of actually wearing masks, were significant threats to morale in the trenches of both sides.

By far the most portentous military invention to appear during the Somme fighting was the track-mounted fighting vehicle. As already noted, the War Office had dropped the idea of land battleships after half-hearted tests with a caterpillar tractor in February 1915. But a small band of persistent enthusiasts had refused to let the matter rest.

Among the more thoughtful responses to the failure of the allied spring offensives that year was a memorandum to the British authorities from an engineer acting as press officer with the BEF, Lieutenant-Colonel E.D. Swinton. Swinton's thesis, 'The Need for Machine-Gun Destroyers', noting the performance of caterpillar tractors he had observed pulling heavy artillery in France, added fresh impetus to a landships committee formed by Winston Churchill.

Churchill's committee, initially an Admiralty enterprise but soon extended to accommodate renewed army interest, arranged further tractor trials. They were encouraging. The outcome was a contract, placed in July with a Lincoln engineering firm, for an experimental armoured machine on tracks, capable of crossing trenches and surmounting parapets.

In September, the first model, dubbed 'Little Willie', was completed. A few months later, a much improved prototype, 'Big

Willie', emerged for trials. Designed principally by William Tritton, managing director of the manufacturers, and Lieutenant W. G. Wilson, a naval engineer, Big Willie was of rhomboid shape, jutting at the prow and falling away at the back, with two fixed turrets and a large sponson on either side of the hull.

Its most revolutionary feature was that, whereas Little Willie and its commercial ancestors rested on their tracks, the tracks of Big Willie ran right round the body.

The vehicle was, indeed, remarkable. Eight feet high, rather more in width, with an overall length of about thirty-three feet, its flat sides and lack of windows (vision was through narrow, inconspicuous prisms) gave it the appearance of some huge, distorted cistern. Its loaded weight, more than twenty-eight tons, was propelled at a lugubrious 3·7 m.p.h. by a 105 h.p. Daimler engine. In each turret was a machine gun, and in each sponson a six-pounder. The whole was armoured to resist bullet fire from ten yards or further.

Apart from a commander and driver, Big Willie's crew comprised four gunners and two gearsmen, the latter to throw the tracks in and out of gear at the direction of the driver – by which method the machine was steered. The only communication with accompanying troops or vehicles was by semaphore. Access for the occupants was by a manhole on top and doors in the sides and rear.

In the early weeks of 1916, Big Willie was demonstrated on a specially prepared obstacle course at Hatfield. The machine met all the tests set for it, crossing trenches up to ten feet wide, climbing parapets of four feet, lumbering through craters and boggy streams. Approval, however, was by no means unanimous among the viewing dignitaries, who included the King, Kitchener, political leaders and a large audience of generals.

Broadly, the politicians, led by Lloyd George, were enthusiastic; Kitchener and the generals, sceptical. The King was agreeably impressed. Hopefully, the production team awaited a mass order. To its disappointment, the War Office requested a meagre forty vehicles.

In keeping with the secrecy surrounding the new device, a name was sought to explain its shape and size in transit. The word 'tank' was adopted as suitably ambiguous.

Big Willie now became the mark 1 tank.

Since its six-pounder guns pronounced it chiefly a destroyer of installations and artillery, it was felt by the tank enthusiasts that a complementary version should be produced, armed exclusively with machine guns to cope with enemy infantry. The two types –

'male' with the heavier guns, 'female' with the lighter weapons – should move in pairs for mutual protection. Thanks largely to Lloyd George, the initial production order was raised to 100 vehicles, and later 150. Swinton was assigned the task of training a Tank Corps.

Recruiting began slowly, hindered by the very secrecy of the project. Prospective volunteers from other arms had to be approached personally. Once enlisted, rumour quickly coloured their activities. To the rest of the troops, the embryonic Tank Corps was 'Fred Karno's Army'. There was some truth in it. For a long time its six companies, each of twenty-five theoretical tanks, had no real tanks to train on; nor was a training course quickly found. With the arrival of the first machines came the problems to be expected from an entirely novel weapon, for which tactics remained as yet unexplored.

Two views prevailed on the immediate future of the Tank Corps. Swinton advised the deferment of tank action until familiarization and methodology were more advanced, and the number of machines could be much increased. The best way to exploit the new service, in his opinion, was to reserve it for an overwhelming

112

surprise attack. That meant keeping it away from the battle front while a substantial force was assembled.

Haig disagreed.

Apprised of the Big Willie trials at Hatfield, the C-in-C had shown interest. Paradoxically, his interest, contrasting with the negative reaction of other generals, did Swinton no service, for Haig insisted on having tanks in France as soon as the first companies were ready.

It was possible to argue that experience of action would provide the Tank Corps with valuable data for its training programme. It was impossible to deny that once action had been joined the secret would be out, sold short to hurry a few early vehicles to the front.

Both Lloyd George, now war minister, and the French authorities, who had started tank production on their own account, supported Swinton's view that the battle debut of the tank should be deferred. But Haig was adamant. The first days of the Somme offensive, with their terrible losses and slender gains, made any new weapon seem desirable. The number of tanks to be had did not greatly worry Haig, who saw them as morale raisers rather than war winners.

By the end of August, two companies of tanks – sixty, including spares – had been shipped to France and stationed near Abbeville, inland of the Somme estuary.

The crews were incompletely trained. Tactics, so far as they existed, were extremely vague. Time needed for practical preparations, especially infantry liaison, was wasted giving pointless demonstrations to inquisitive staff officers from GHQ. Before a single exercise could be arranged with the infantry, the bemused tank men were bustled into the third great assault of the Somme, the offensive of 15 September.

It was the last chance of a major advance before winter, and Haig, as Rawlinson noted, was 'anxious to have a gamble with all the available troops ... with the object of breaking down German resistance and getting through to Bapaume'. The attack was planned on a ten mile front along the Pozières Ridge from Thiepval to a point at its southern end, Combles. With greater realism than in previous British planning, the new offensive was to proceed in four stages, each attempting a modest gain of a few hundred yards – rather more in the fourth and final push – in the manner of Falkenhayn's phased advance at Verdun.

With his big guns concentrated to a weight of one every thirty yards, Haig unleashed a three day preliminary bombardment, the field artillery providing standing and creeping barrages.

Five corps were mustered in the front line, three of the 4th Army

Trench oddity – a captured German wearing body armour.

and two, including the Canadian Corps, from the Reserve Army originally formed under General Gough. This gave twelve divisions, one of New Zealanders, to tackle an enemy front line held by six and a half German divisions. Forty-nine tanks were detailed to the attack, forty-two with the 4th Army, seven with the Reserve Army. At best, their contribution to the outcome could only be marginal, and Britain's tank enthusiasts had continued to lobby against their premature engagement.

Churchill wrote later:

> I was so shocked at the proposal to expose this tremendous secret to the enemy upon such a petty scale and as a mere makeweight to what I was sure could only be an indecisive operation, that I sought an interview with the prime minister. ... He received me in the most friendly manner and listened so patiently to my appeal that I thought I had succeeded in convincing him. But if this were so, he did not make his will effective, for on 15 September the first tanks went into action.

The manner of their deployment proved as controversial as the fact that they were used at all. In mass, even the modest force on the Somme would have formed a substantial armoured spearhead somewhere on the line. Instead, the thirty-six machines which actually reached the line without breaking down or becoming ditched were distributed along the front in small groups.

This was hard on the tank men but made sense to Haig's infantry commanders, who looked to the vehicles, albeit with dubiety, to deal with the German strongposts which dotted the defences.

That the tanks astonished the enemy was vouchsafed in his reports. A German war correspondent at the front described the scene luridly:

> When the German pickets crept out of their dug-outs in the mist of the morning and stretched their necks to look for the English, their blood chilled. Mysterious monsters were crawling towards them over the craters. ... The monsters approached slowly, hobbling, rolling and rocking, but they approached. Nothing impeded them. A supernatural force seemed to impel them forward. Someone in the trenches said, 'The devil is coming', and the word was passed along the line. Tongues of flame leapt from the sides of the iron caterpillars ... the English infantry came in waves behind.

Within the tanks, fumes and noise from the big engine in the centre were barely sufferable. Tossed from side to side over bumpy ground, sweating beneath goggles and leather 'anti-bruise' helmets, the crews struggled to hold their unwieldy ships on course, praying that the sparking plugs would not give up or a leaky exhaust pipe asphyxiate anyone.

In contrast to the robot-like, depersonalized exterior, the interior of the vehicles was a veritable hell's kitchen of men, gun mechanisms, ammunition, drums of oil and grease, signalling equipment and soldiers' kit. Jammed somewhere amid the rest, were thirty tins of food, sixteen loaves, cheese, tea, sugar, milk and the iron rations for each tank. There was also a basket of carrier pigeons, hopefully to bear progress reports to headquarters as the machines advanced.

Many Germans in forward positions ran from the path of the vehicles. Others stayed bravely to toss grenades at the lumbering giants. Indeed, a few approached with such temerity that the tank men raised their hatches and shot at them with pistols. Everywhere, Haig's infantry pressed forward doggedly. According to the official German history, 15 September was 'a very heavy day of fighting, even by Somme standards'. For a moment, it was admitted, the defence was in considerable peril, but the arrival of six extra

German divisions stiffened resistance, and the ultimate British gain did not match expectations.

The tank contribution was of varied effectiveness.

Half the machines which had reached the front failed to get under way at zero hour. Five of those which did advance bogged down in the subsequent action. Others encountered mechanical breakdowns in the course of their missions, or were knocked out by shell fire. Less than a dozen actually played any part in the overrunning of strong-points and trenches.

Unable to determine their own tactics, some tank crews were assigned improbable tasks by infantry commanders. On one sector, four vehicles were sent into a wood.

Of the successes, the most notable was the performance of seven tanks in the 41st Division's attack on the village of Flers, the vicinity of the deepest British penetration. Four sustained direct hits in the advance, but three rumbled on for a mile or so to the defended fringe of the village, brushing aside machine guns and smashing fortifications. One, commanded by a Captain Hastie, drove right through the main street, accompanied by a party of infantry.

On the whole, the first tank action of history was not attended by remarkable achievement. If the invention had been exposed with imprudent haste, at least its potential had scarcely been emphasized. Indeed, despite the initial shock of the German troops their commanders were unimpressed, and Germany took no serious steps to produce its own tanks.

British troops, on the other hand, were enheartened. At last the long-suffering trench soldier sensed he had found an ally, however imperfect in its present shape, against the unholy partnership of wire and machine gun. His reaction was touchingly affectionate.

'"Old Mother Hubbard" they called her, and lots of other funny names,' recalled a wounded Territorial of the first tank he encountered. 'It was a circus, my word! She came bumping out of the fog at one end of the line and bumped into it again at the other. The last I saw of her was nosing down a shell crater like a huge hippopotamus with a crowd of Tommies cheering behind.'

Haig had seen enough within a few hours to want a lot more tanks. Two days after the commencement of the battle, he sent his deputy chief of staff to England to urge the production of a further thousand vehicles. It was, perhaps, the most positive outcome of the September offensive.

The rest was all too familiar.

116 By the end of the first phase of the attack, heavy casualties plus

the inability to capture vital tactical positions had made it evident
that the operation would not achieve its object. By 18 September,
rain was falling steadily, reviving the usual winter quagmire.
'Nothing could exceed the depression of the scene,' wrote a visitor.
'A flat country enveloped in fog and soaked in rain; practically
every house destroyed; trees without branches, and the ground so
pitted with shell holes that there was sometimes barely standing
room between them. Mud everywhere.'

Unshaken in his belief that 'steady offensive pressure' must
result in the enemy's 'complete overthrow', Haig refused to bow to
the elements. By the end of the month the battle had been reduced
to short scrambles through a sea of churned earth, interspersed
with longer periods of exhaustion. On the 27th, Thiepval was
finally captured, now a mere heap of rubble and human bones.

Five days later the weather broke completely. Movement of the
huge quantity of guns and ammunition to a drier part of the line
would have been impossible, even if desirable. A dozen horses were
now needed to shift a field gun; only pack mules could move with
ammunition; the mud clung and balled so persistently on men's
boots that unladen messengers sometimes collapsed from exertion.
Conversion to the doctrines of mass and attrition had bound Haig
to his own bloody anvil.

Against the better judgement of most infantry commanders, one
more big attack was planned in October, but, though some advances
were attempted, it was increasingly a problem of reaching the
starting line rather than of driving back the enemy. November saw

some gains around Ancre, against the stubborn defences of the
northern sector. They represented the last toils of the Somme in
1916. It had begun to snow between rainstorms. Operations were
halted for the winter.

The great battles of the Somme had cost the British about 420,000
casualties, the French nearly 200,000. Territorially, the Germans
had been squeezed back on about thirty miles of front, in some
sectors insignificantly, elsewhere up to seven miles. It was a minor
dent in enemy-held France, won at such a painfully protracted
slog that the Germans had been able to construct new defences as
needed in the process. Nowhere had there been a breakthrough or
exploitable victory.

Trench warfare had altered chiefly in that it had grown more
dangerous.

The policy of offensives of attrition, initiated by Falkenhayn at

Verdun and pursued by Haig in his later advances, had balanced
the ratio of losses between attacked and attackers in major battles
on the Western Front. The tremendous barrages used to support
attacks, combined with an increasing reluctance on both sides to
yield any ground, had much reduced the comparative impunity of
the trench defender.

The French had actually lost more men in their defence of Verdun
than had their assailants, while German casualties on the Somme
almost equalled allied losses. As a result, both sides had been bled
white of seasoned troops. In a letter to Joffre in November, Haig
succinctly described the outcome of the Somme fighting in human
terms:

A very considerable proportion of the personnel in my divisions
consists now of almost untrained young officers and men, and to bring
my units up to strength I have still to receive during the winter a large
number of those with even less training. My armies will in fact consist
of what I can only describe as raw material, and without intensive
training throughout the winter they cannot be fit for an offensive next
spring.

Chapter 7

Succour,
Medical and Spiritual

The failure of the Somme offensive brought a few months of quiet on the front, during which the trench soldier's worst enemies were once more the elements. The quagmire on the Somme exceeded even the conditions of the previous two winters. British troops sank literally to their armpits, as helpless as cattle in a bog until their mates rescued them.

That the German lines were as bad, and morale sometimes worse, was indicated by the experience of a Somerset Regiment sergeant while checking forward wire entanglements.

According to his commanding officer, he had made some headway 'when he became hopelessly bogged and unable to move. He was found by a party of five Boches who proceeded to pull him out. He, of course, expected to be taken to the Hun lines, but ... they informed him that they were *his* prisoners and demanded to be taken to our trenches ... On the way they picked up another of our men, also bogged, and took him back with them.'

Frosts stiffened the morass, but brought their own agonies.

An Australian soldier on the Somme told how the ice in shell holes was melted to obtain water when supplies from the rear failed. 'An axe would be the means of filling the dixies [iron stewing pots] with lumps of ice. We used it for tea several days until one chap noticed a pair of boots sticking out, and discovered they were attached to a body ... Many people say it is the coldest winter they have ever experienced.'

The mud and the cold, on top of the strain of the offensive, induced widespread weariness. An officer who awoke after dozing off to find his dug-out in total darkness, although it was daytime, heard his men digging and realized that the entrance had been smothered by a shell burst. So profound was his exhaustion that he had slept through the explosion which entombed him.

Opposite An army chaplain reads burial service in a trench.

Tired, frozen, lice ridden, often cut off from fresh food supplies, the Somme survivor had reason to consider the fact that he was still alive after two years of trench warfare an ironic consolation. For some, the prospect of oblivion seemed merciful. Others pondered the possibilities of injury. A ticket to Blighty bought with a modest wound was a favourite trench fantasy. But nobody envied 'the poor blighter who copped it bad'. What happened to him was something seldom talked about.

The Boer War had seen a rapid expansion of the army's medical facilities. At its end, about twenty-one thousand hospital beds had been in service, a huge number as it then seemed. Twice as many could have been filled by a single day's fighting at the height of the conflict on the Western Front. Not only for sheer numbers, but also for the fearfulness of the injuries, nothing approaching the casualties

of the trench war had been known in medical history.

Britain entered the war with a thousand army doctors. Dramatically as the strength of the Royal Army Medical Corps was increased during the conflict, unsparingly as its staff worked, arrangements for coping with the human wreckage of the great trench battles proved tragically inadequate.

The Ancre valley, November 1916.

123

Melting snow to obtain
water, Neulette, 1917.

Some sense of the medical crisis following the opening of the
Somme campaign is conveyed in the recollections of a young surgeon
then at a casualty station between Albert and Amiens. It had been
set up with tented accommodation for an anticipated thousand
patients on one sector during the offensive; it received nearly ten
124   thousand in the first forty-eight hours.

Streams of ambulances a mile long waited to be unloaded ... the whole area of the camp, a field of five or six acres, was completely covered with stretchers placed side by side, each with its suffering or dying man on it. Orderlies went about giving water, and dressing wounds where possible. We surgeons were hard at it in the operating theatre, a good hut holding four tables. Occasionally we made a brief look around to select from the thousands of patients those few we had time to save. It was terrible.

The writer had been qualified for twelve months.

Many medical graduates had volunteered for the RAMC in the expectation that the conflict would be short and offer valuable experience. 'War,' recalled one, 'did not suggest unnamed horrors, but to a young surgeon implied useful employment in his own profession while doing his duty.' In the event, it provided both unique surgical experience *and* 'unnamed horrors'.

With the abrupt and chaotic retreat from Mons had come the first realization that clinical problems on the Western Front were to be very different from those of the Boer War. In the light of South African experience, medical officers were at first instructed not to interfere with 'clean' bullet wounds. But, when patients began dying of arm and leg injuries, it quickly became clear that contamination from the dung-laden soil of Flanders and northern France was a far more serious matter than the relatively sterile conditions of Natal and the Transvaal.

In particular, anaerobic bacteria, gas-forming organisms prevalent in the mud and muck, caused a deadly infection known as gas gangrene (not a reference to man-made war gas) which defeated all preventive measures until 1918.

As a consequence, army surgeons, often of very short experience, were confronted repeatedly with the daunting choice between risking fatal infection in their patients or amputating limbs which should otherwise have been saved.

Another characteristic of the new war was the complexity of injuries inflicted by high explosive shells, hand grenades and machine guns – weapons bearing little relation to the high velocity rifles of the Boers. Jagged fragments of shell and bomb casing embedded not only themselves, but earth and filthy clothing, deep in their victims, where discovery was difficult. With antibiotics unknown, and the principles of surgical toilet of wounds not yet endorsed by common usage, antiseptics were the chief, and largely futile, hope against infection.

The first winter of the static war brought new implacable diseases to the attention of the doctors. So-called 'trench foot' and 'trench fever' became as dreaded as they were ubiquitous. Neither responded to any tried form of treatment. Indeed the latter, in many cases very serious, remained unexplained until the war's end, when it was found to be a louse-borne infection.

Meanwhile, the evolution of fixed lines of trenches enabled the medical service at least to organize on a fairly settled basis. In general, it worked like this: in the forefront of casualty evacuation were the regimental stretcher-bearers (infantry soldiers), who picked the wounded from the field and carried them to the regimental aid post (RAP). Situated in the front line, the RAP was supervised by the regimental medical officer.

From here casualties passed, either by stretcher or as walking cases, rearward to the dressing stations: first, the advanced dressing station; then, for more detailed attention, to a main dressing station. Serious cases were now transported by ambulance to the casualty clearing station (CCS), while others made their way there by hitching lifts, or as best they could.

Perhaps seven miles or so from the battle front, beyond the range of enemy artillery, the CCS was the most advanced link in the system with planned provision for major surgery and the retention of the badly hurt – in effect, a field hospital. By road or ambulance train, its patients were fed back to base hospitals near the Channel, whence, when appropriate they were shipped to England.

The system worked reasonably well until caught by the gory wash of major actions, then it was simply swamped. At such times, the stretcher-bearers laboured ceaselessly. In wet periods it could

'Trench feet', one of the scourges of life in the front line.

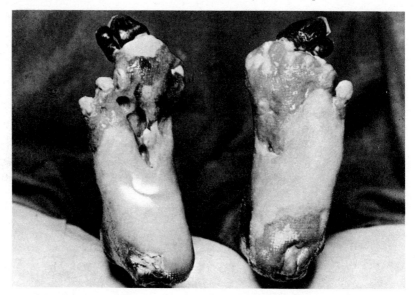

take half a dozen or more of them to carry one casualty through deep mud at a snail's pace, unable to run or take cover as the shells fell. Justifiably, the stretcher-bearers were much admired by their comrades.

Also highly respected were most front line doctors, the regimental medical officers whose determination to apply civilized attitudes to disaster where civilized standards had otherwise disappeared often meant more to fighting soldiers than actual healing skills. Too frequently, the latter were palpably superfluous:

> I was summoned to the telephonists' dug-out [after a direct shell hit near Ypres] where three men had chosen to remain ... every trace of the bodies above their waists had vanished. It seemed in a way foolish to worry about what remained, but it was felt that the legs had to be decently buried, so I carefully extracted as much as I could. ...

In quieter times, that particular MO held his surgery in a converted pigsty and learned to ride a horse for his more distant rounds. In the attempt, he fell off and was concussed.

When operations intensified, the front line doctor presided over the RAP, commonly a dug-out in the forward trenches. Badly wounded men were spread out on the ground for treatment; others huddled against the earth walls. 'There is blood everywhere: all other smells are drowned by its stench. Fumes from a coke brazier fill the place ... and bits of clothing, equipment and dirty bloody dressings.'

A German aid post, though deeper and better built, presented an equally fearful picture after battle: 'On descending about forty steps one was in a large floored and timbered chamber ... filled with dead and wounded. ... A big bevy of rats squeaked and scuttled away from their feast on the dead bodies on the floor. The stench was indescribably abominable.'

Overleaf Advanced dressing station, France. Picture by Henry Tonks.

Further behind the British lines, the doctors at the CCS were removed from danger but no less overwhelmed by its cruel effects. With the incessant rumble of gunfire in the background, the surgical teams could often anticipate a fresh flood of casualties by ominous surges of the barrage. They could then prepare to work virtually non-stop until near collapse. 'After three hours' sleep, I had to operate continuously for another twenty-one hours. That night I was called up after only three more hours' sleep. My physical state was such that I was at first unable to stand, and it took some little time before I could collect my faculties.'

The need to limit resources of skill and energy to those patients with the best hopes of recovery was distressing. The eminent

127

The endless procession. Wounded being evacuated near Ginchy, 1916. German prisoners carry an officer of the Grenadier Guards on a stretcher.

surgeon, Sir Geoffrey Keynes, then a young MO, told how he was tormented by the moribund ward at a CCS, where patients classified as 'probably beyond surgical aid' were left to die.

Like others, he gave up precious resting time to steal into the ward and administer 'unofficial' treatment to its hapless inmates, often successfully. Since most of those given up as beyond help were suffering primarily from shock and loss of blood, the more knowledgeable use of transfusions as the war progressed saved many lives.

In 1915, blood transfusion and intravenous fluid replacements were barely considered by the medical authorities.

Occasionally, in critical cases, a blood donor would be called for among the lightly wounded (sometimes on promise of an extra fortnight's leave in Blighty) and linked directly by tube to the patient. Grouping was a calculated risk based on the premise that one man in two was a 'universal donor', while the flow of blood was assured by the higher blood pressure of the less severely hurt soldier.

Later, the combination of preliminary grouping and a new technique using sodium citrate to prevent blood coagulation, hugely extended the scope for life-saving surgery. Indirect trans-

130

fusion was introduced to some CCSs in 1917. With its help, and the use of a spinal analgesic, surgeons commonly performed successful major operations single-handed. Abdominal surgery, at first discouraged by the medical authorities, was considerably advanced by the determined enterprise of individual surgeons, as were brain, chest and facial surgery.

A serious problem at times of heavy fighting was the continuous pressure to shift post-operative patients hastily from the CCS to make room for new intakes. The shock of crude transportation ruined the recuperative chances of many. Even ambulance trains, the quickest and smoothest link with the base hospitals, were rough on the badly injured, who travelled in cattle trucks adapted for stretchers. Shunting was sometimes so erratic that couplings were smashed. Where negligence or gross incompetence was involved, engine drivers were arrested.

The base hospitals accommodated huge numbers of men. One, at Boulogne, had more than twenty thousand beds, yet still the need for proper care was unsatisfied. 'The convoys keep coming in, two or three a night,' wrote a base nurse. 'Sometimes in the middle of the night we have to turn people out of bed and make them sleep on the floor to make room for more seriously ill from the line. We have heaps of gassed cases at present.'

From the beginning of the war, at least five hundred female nurses, the QAs (Queen Alexander's Royal Army Nursing Corps), had served with the BEF. This number was to multiply tenfold before the armistice. Some found their way to field hospitals, but the majority worked at the bases, coping valiantly with conditions far removed from their normally genteel backgrounds.

'Never in my life have I been so absolutely filthy,' one QA informed her mother. 'I am Sister, VAD and orderly all in one. After (quite apart from the nursing) I have stoked the stove all night, done two or three rounds of bedpans, kept the kettles going, prepared feeds on exceedingly black oil stoves and refilled them from the steam kettles, literally wallowing in paraffin all the time, I feel as if I have been dragged through the gutter.'

To contend with the excessive work, nurses began their ward duties as early as 3 a.m. In winter, heating provisions were so deplorable that water taps froze and staff wore their overcoats in the wards.

From the base hospitals, patients either passed to England for long-term treatment or release from service, or were returned as fit to their BEF units. Siegfried Sassoon, who received a bullet through the upper part of his body, was among those shipped from

base hospital to Blighty where, on Charing Cross station, 'a woman handed me a bunch of flowers and a leaflet by the Bishop of London who earnestly advised me to lead a clean life and attend Holy Communion.'

As the shortage of trained soldiers increased, medical boards were urged to speed patients back to duty in maximum numbers. As a result, the image of the medical authorities became tarnished by a seemingly harsh and unsympathetic attitude towards convalescent troops.

It was not improved in some cases by the diligence with which certain old-school MOs co-operated with the disciplinary authorities in reporting self-inflicted wounds and other alleged attempts 'to swing the lead'. Such doctors, however, were overshadowed at the front by younger colleagues with a new and compassionate view of battle stresses.

Significantly, Captain Noel Chevasse, one of two RAMC officers to win the VC and Bar in the war, also won the disapproval of a court martial for sympathizing with a man who had shot himself in the hand at Loos. Chevasse had trimmed away the incriminating scorch marks in an attempt, frustrated as it turned out, to conceal the incident.

Indeed, perhaps the most fundamental of all medical advances in the war was the acceptance for the first time of various nervous reactions to battle conditions as clinical problems. Though 'shell

shock', the general label for mental distress, seems crude in retro-spect, it was considerably more enlightened than its earlier designation, 'lack of moral fibre'.

The impression that the army chaplains made on the fighting soldier varied according not only to the religious predisposition of the individual man, and the personal qualities of the chaplain, but also the instructions issued by head chaplains in different areas.

'At the beginning of the war,' according to one cleric, 'chaplains were not allowed in the front line. But it was soon found that this had to be countermanded. It militated against the influence of the chaplain if he did not share the dangers of the men and confined his activities to times when they came out of the line.' On the other hand, there appears to have been no general directive obliging chaplains to work in the front line. Rather, head chaplains used their influence at discretion.

Certainly, a number of padres endeared themselves to the troops by their indifference to personal peril and discomfort. Among them, the Reverend Theodore Bailey Hardy won the VC, DSO and MC in a period of twelve months, refusing to leave the front even when invited to become a chaplain to the King. He was killed in action at the age of fifty-four.

Other chaplains were remembered affectionately in soldiers'
reminiscences. A rifleman in a Scottish regiment recalled how,
defending his position against a German advance, he heard digging,
looked up, and saw a chaplain wielding a spade beside him. 'He
smiles and says as he turns a sod, "Get on with your work, soldier,
I'm making a bit of cover for you".'

The same chaplain was killed shortly afterwards.

On the whole, however, first-hand accounts of trench warfare suggest a conspicuous absence of padres in the forward lines – a curious omission when, as Bishop W. C. Wand (himself a World War I chaplain) noted later, the war was 'making even the most careless face the issues of life and death'; and when 'the fundamental questions of religion and philosophy had to be tackled afresh'.

Writing of *The Sheep that were not Fed*, C. E. Montague expressed

The Square at Ypres, 1916.
Overleaf Home from home. A London coffee stall in service at Auchonvillers, during fighting on the Ancre, 1916.

the conviction that, consciously or unconsciously, men at the front acquired a receptiveness to spiritual values which presented the churches with a unique opportunity.

> Nobody used it: the tide in the affairs of churches flowed its best, but no church came to take it. Instead, as if chance had planned a kind of satiric practical epigram, came the brigade chaplain. As soon as his genial bulk hove in sight, and his cheery robustious chaff began blowing about, the shy and uncouth muse of our savage theology unfolded her wings and flew away. Once more the talk was all footer and rations and scragging the Kaiser.

That chaplains were in attendance at field hospitals, and sometimes at RAPs, was well attested, but it seemed evident that at least Protestant padres were not encouraged to linger in the most dangerous areas. Sensible as such a ruling might have been from a military standpoint, it interposed a gulf between the average padre and the fighting man which few hastened to cross once line duty was over.

If a general exception is to be found among contemporary observations, it is in respect of Roman Catholic priests.

'Roman Catholic chaplains,' wrote Robert Graves, 'were not only permitted to visit posts of danger, but definitely enjoined to be wherever fighting was.' As another infantry officer saw it, Catholic padres were the most 'effective'. They 'succeeded in getting quite reasonably close to the enemy, and sometimes got into danger'.

Just how large a part the efforts of army chaplains, or indeed the religiosity of the troops themselves, played in the trench war can never be truly told. Contrary to popular misconception, the great mass of people was far from devout in the Edwardian era. It may be, as one prelate has put it, that 'the period just before the war was the heyday of religious observance in the West', but that speaks more of the subsequent decline than any overwhelming celebration at the time.

Working men were respectful of the Church, as of other strongholds of the 'establishment', but they did not rush to fill churches. A study at the beginning of the century indicated that, even in the cathedral city of York, only twenty-eight per cent of the population normally went to church. Of those who did, a substantial section was middle class and men were outnumbered by women.

The middle and upper classes, which provided the army's officers, were most united in their support of the Church. Religion was an important part of their youthful instruction, and its regular observance compulsory at public schools. Haig personified that portion of the officer cadre which carried its faith unequivocally through the war.

Another portion was dubious. John Baynes, an officer who has based a study of morale on Western Front survivors from his own regiment, found that not more than half the officers he questioned were definite that religious faith was a help in the trenches.

Among other ranks, the proportion was much lower. Robert Graves asserted that, 'Hardly one soldier in a hundred was inspired by religious feeling of even the crudest kind'. In a unit where service before battle was optional, 'Very few attended,' according to one member, 'and those who did were mostly not very stout soldiers.'

Baynes is more conservative. According to his figures, one ranker in every two attached no importance to religion in the trenches. Nevertheless, while only a small minority actually claimed religion was an important help in the line, Baynes estimated that a substantial number received intermittent support from it in some form.

'Many would laugh at religion one day and pray most sincerely the next, particularly if under heavy shell fire. My estimate is that forty per cent reacted in this way.'

More striking in the trenches than overt religion was the brotherly bond between soldier and soldier, the sense of comradeship which had spawned the 'pals' battalions, which had burgeoned through training and was consummated in action. Again and again, men shouldered the burdens of weaker mates, risked their lives to rescue comrades, even tried to help the families of dead pals.

Such was the military tradition best exemplified by the trench soldier – not the bloody and vengeful deeds celebrated in chauvinistic literature, but the sharing of hardship, the sacrifice of brother for brother.

Chapter 8

The Road to Passchendaele

By the end of 1916, serious anxieties about the conduct of the war had led to changes of leadership in each of the major nations involved on the Western Front. Falkenhayn, tarnished by his ultimate failure at Verdun, was replaced at the end of August by two German officers who had won victories in Russia: Field-Marshal Paul von Hindenburg and General Erich Ludendorff. They were formidable if incongruous partners.

Hindenburg, an aged military aristocrat summoned from retirement in 1914, was a living caricature of a nineteenth-century Prussian officer and Junker. Heavy jowled, magnificently paunched, proudly upright, he radiated a serene dignity, an austere and unwavering loyalty to the Fatherland, which made him the object of almost neurotic national reverence.

While Hindenburg, as chief of the general staff, provided the grand image and stability, Ludendorff supplied the brains as *de facto* commander of the field force. A restless, aggressive careerist, he looked, despite the eyeglass and Prussian haircut he affected, more the product, as indeed he was, of a bourgeois family of commerce.

In France, Joffre at last succumbed to mounting dissatisfaction with his painful and seemingly unproductive attrition strategy. December saw his replacement by General Robert Nivelle, an officer who had caught the public's imagination by a successful counter-offensive at Verdun in the autumn.

An unknown artillery colonel of fifty-eight at the outbreak of hostilities, Nivelle appeared as an ageing upstart to many of his fellow officers. His promotion over the heads of such senior commanders as Foch and Pétain was largely due to the exposition of a method he designated 'mass of manoeuvre', by which he proposed to drive 'violently' through the German lines in terrific strength, overwhelming the enemy at a stroke.

The scheme was as blind to the fate of past offensives as it proved irresistible to a despairing French government. Nivelle proclaimed the day of swift victory.

Britain, too, had shuffled her leadership.

In June, Kitchener, travelling to Russia, had been drowned when the warship *Hampshire* had struck a mine, leaving Lloyd George to take over as war minister. The tragedy of the Somme assured further changes. Criticism of the generals, and Asquith's endorsement of their methods, became widespread, culminating in December with the removal of the prime minister and the elevation in his place of the sharp and mercurial war minister.

Opposite General Erich Ludendorff.

141

Field-Marshal Paul von Hindenburg.

For a moment, Lloyd George's distrust of the British generals, with their unimaginative confidence in stereotyped attacks, threatened the kind of shake-up seen in France and Germany. But Haig and his colleagues had powerful friends; while the new premier, for all his critical acumen, offered no acceptable alternatives to their strategies.

Finally, with the French government, he fell back on Nivelle as a means of breaking from Haig's and Joffre's policies.

In the ensuing struggle of personalities, Haig found himself not only confronted by his government's acceptance of Nivelle's plan, but with a top level Anglo-French intrigue to subordinate him to the French general. The outcome was a compromise, by which Haig would broadly conform to Nivelle's instructions with freedom to implement his own methods in the British sector.

The scheme, detailed early in 1917, involved a massive surprise attack by French forces towards Laon, between the Somme and the Aisne, while the BEF extended its responsibilities south of the Somme to release French troops for a further blow in Champagne. By way of distraction, the British were to make 'a powerful offensive'

142

General Robert Nivelle, Joffre's successor.

a few days earlier, between Bapaume and Arras, near the international boundary.

Plans for Nivelle's master stroke were still in preparation when Ludendorff made his first move.

If some of the assumptions behind it were questionable, it did not, like the French project, perpetuate the illusion of a decisive victory in the trench war. Ludendorff expected Britain to be defeated at sea. According to German naval experts, unrestricted U-boat warfare, starting in February, would force the island adversary out of the war within twelve months. True, it would almost certainly bring the USA in on the allied side, but, concluded Ludendorff, American military aid would be too little, too late, and more than offset by the decline of Russian power.

In fact, the Russian revolution – precipitated in March by enormous war losses, a corrupt royal *entourage* and deep-seated moral issues – led swiftly to the collapse of that nation as a war power, in contrast with which America was to achieve the modest provision of four divisions in Europe by December.

It followed from Ludendorff's reasoning that his task on the 143

British troops in a
captured German
trench on the Ancre,
1917.

Western Front was to stand on the defensive until such time – probably the onset of next winter – as Britain was reduced to indigence by the U-boat campaign, and the redeployment of German forces from the east gave him the numerical superiority to crush France.

To this end the Germans had been busy constructing a new fortified line behind the Somme battlefield. Known in Germany as 'the Siegfried line', to the allies as 'the Hindenburg line', this described the chord of the bulging German arc from near Arras south to the Aisne, considerably reducing the frontage.

At first Ludendorff had regarded the new line as a precautionary measure, a resort in the event of possible allied successes in the spring. Then he hit on a more original idea. Instead of waiting for the enemy to attack, he would retire to the Siegfried line on the very eve of the campaign season, thus disrupting the enemy's preparations. His instructions for the withdrawal were as ruthless as the notion was brilliant.

The entire zone between the existing fighting line and the new position – an area averaging about twenty miles in depth across a sixty-five mile front – was to be made a desert: its towns and villages demolished, its woods and orchards erased, its wells blocked or polluted.

Demolitions began on 9 March and the troops started to move back a week later, ripping up roads and laying booby traps. Extraordinarily, the allies virtually ignored the withdrawal, which was accomplished before Nivelle would believe that the Germans had voluntarily abandoned ten times as much ground as the British and French had captured in 1916. Within a few days, Ludendorff had saved half his divisions on the sector for reserve use, much improved the position of the rest, and left his enemies to attack across miles of open wasteland.

Any glimmer of success which had reposed in Nivelle's scheme was aborted.

The main French attack opened on 16 April. The weather was execrable; the Germans, amply alerted by the huge scale of the build-up and Nivelle's loquacity, were waiting; the preliminary bombardment had failed to destroy their machine-gun posts.

Within hours, the massive attack force was floundering in the familiar trench war predicament. Nine days of agonizing perseverance and courage achieved little but 187,000 French casualties. Medical services at the front completely broke down. In the first week of May, what remained of the offensive ground to a despairing 146 halt, and an alarmed council of French ministers prepared to

supersede Nivelle as commander-in-chief by Marshal Pétain.

Thousands of Frenchmen reacted more radically. Indiscipline, aggravated by poor service conditions in rear areas, spread rapidly through the ranks. Among its other manifestations, infantry units refused to go to the front, troops held anti-war demonstrations, railways were disrupted, instances of arson and stone throwing occurred, while red flags and revolutionary songs were much in evidence. Altogether, there were 119 cases of mutiny in 54 divisions, leading eventually to 23,385 convictions by courts martial and 432 death sentences (all but 55 were commuted and the prisoners sent to penal colonies).

As Pétain struggled to rally his forces, Haig's armies assumed the full burden of the offensive.

Since the Somme offensive, the BEF had grown in men and materials. By the end of 1916, Britain and the dominions had 56   147

divisions on the Western Front (France had 101, Belgium 12). By March 1917, six more British divisions had arrived, all of the Territorial Force. They were, as Haig complained, lacking in experience; but so by now was a large proportion of the forces of all belligerents.

Deteriorating rail transport in France was a problem (Sir Eric Geddes, a former manager of the North Eastern Railway, was put in

charge of reorganizing the system behind the British front) but the
flow of munitions had much improved. In the last quarter of 1916
the production of shells in Britain had stood at nearly 21 million as
opposed to less than 4,500,000 in the first quarter. Hand grenades
were leaving the factories at the rate of 250,000 a week, while the
year had brought an extra 33,500 machine guns and 5,190 mortars
to British troops.

Infantry with bayonets
fixed wait to move
forward near St
Quentin after the
German withdrawal to
the Hindenberg Line,
1917.

If short on training in many units, the BEF faced the 1917 offensive better armed, especially in artillery, than when it had ventured on the Somme attacks.

On Monday, 9 April, according to Nivelle's plan, the assault had commenced on the British sector. The weather, cold and bright, was to bring sleet and scattered snow later. A war correspondent described the effect on the French downs as that of a delicate watercolour by Turner. From Arras, the line of advance was marked by the River Scarpe. To its north, the 1st Army's immediate objective was Vimy Ridge, a straggling crest where the Artois plateau met the Douai plain.

To the south, the 3rd and 5th Armies aimed for Bullecourt and Cambrai, in a region affected by the German retirement.

The battle of Arras, as the operation became known, got off to a stirring start on most of the thirty mile British front. The most spectacular success was the storming of Vimy Ridge by the Canadian Corps, the first exclusively Canadian victory of the war, and one

which marked its participants as future storm troops. But the deepest penetration was made by the 3rd Army, under Allenby, covering five miles in places on the first day.

Jubilantly, Allenby looked for the breakthrough. Instead, hope was eroded by unseasonable weather and his own repetition of old mistakes. Again, the tanks (the 3rd Army had forty) were split into small groups and used on the wrong ground. Some bogged down immediately. Other crews were confused by poor briefing.

An Australian soldier told how the infantry 'had very soon overtaken the tanks, which were mostly floundering around close in front. Some of them even fired on our own men, but no one knows precisely how many they killed. As it was fatal to hesitate and wait for the tanks, the line advanced alone. As soon as it came in sight of the Huns, the massacre commenced, the enemy lining his parapet and shooting our boys like rabbits.'

The third day proved critical.

Bad weather washed out RFC observations, German reinforcements were arriving, and the British guns were not finding the defensive posts. Still, Allenby behaved on the assumption of breakthrough: 'The Army commander wishes all troops to understand that the 3rd Army is now pursuing a defeated enemy and that risks must be freely taken.' To complete the delusion, he threw in cavalry. A highlander watched them near the front line village of Monchy-le-Preux:

> During a lull in the snowstorm an excited shout was raised that our cavalry were coming up! Sure enough, away behind us, moving quickly in extended order down the slope of Orange Hill, was line upon line of mounted men covering the whole of the hillside as far as we could see. ... It may have been a fine sight, but it was a wicked waste of men and horses, for the enemy immediately opened on them a hurricane of every kind of missile. If the cavalry advanced through us at the trot or canter, they came back at a gallop, including dismounted men and riderless horses. ...
>
> They left numbers of dead and wounded among us, but the horses seem to have suffered most, and for a while after we put bullets into poor brutes that were aimlessly limping about on three legs, or careering madly in their agony like one I saw with the whole of its muzzle blown away.

The cavalry sally was disastrous. A swirling blizzard put out the tanks and caused foot units to lose contact with each other. Two Australian brigades which penetrated the Hindenburg positions were surrounded and one virtually eliminated. The other extricated itself with crippling losses.

On 14 April, Allenby's determination to keep attacking, despite all losses and setbacks, brought a written protest from three of his

generals; and Haig stepped in to call a prompt halt. Fighting was
resumed on the Scarpe and round Bullecourt towards the end of
the month, but the collapse of Nivelle's offensive on the Aisne put a
final stop to the campaign.

The battle of Arras had left 30,000 of Haig's soldiers dead,
128,000 wounded, losses on a scale not far short of Nivelle's. Unlike
Nivelle, however, Haig emerged unscathed.

It had not been the British commander who had made the
sweeping promises. On the contrary, Haig had warned that his
troops needed more training and that his reserves would be over-
stretched. Despite which, the earlier phases of the battle, particularly
Vimy Ridge, appeared as spectacular achievements in the plodding
context of the trench war.

Thus, while Nivelle was discredited and French morale plum-
meted, Haig's credibility survived, as did the spirit of his fighting
troops. With the allied banner on the Western Front firmly in his
own hands, he now turned to the strategy he had favoured before
Nivelle upset his plans: namely, a northern offensive aimed at the
Belgian coast.

With dogged confidence, Haig envisaged a relentless blow from
the Ypres salient towards the region of Passchendaele village, on the

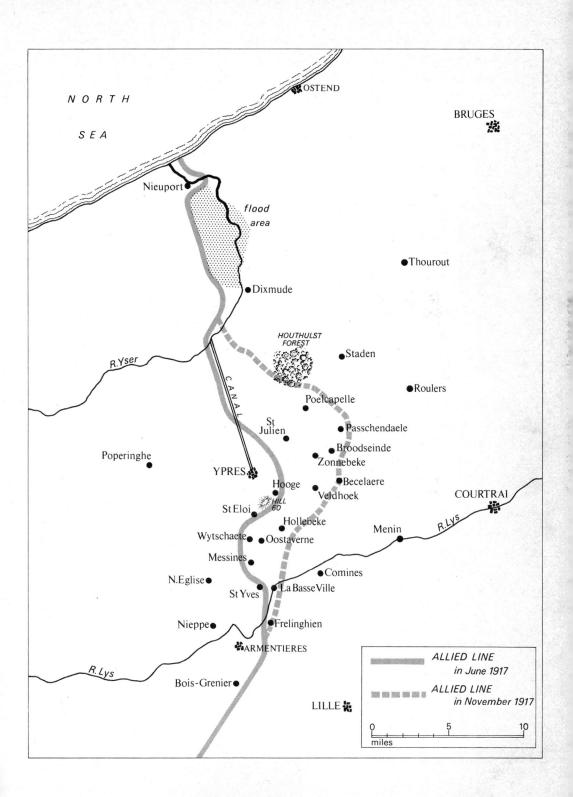

NORTH

SEA

OSTEND

BRUGES

Nieuport

flood area

Thourout

Dixmude

R. Yser

CANAL

HOUTHULST FOREST

Staden

Roulers

Poelcapelle

St Julien

Passchendaele

Broodseinde

Zonnebeke

Poperinghe

YPRES

Hooge

Becelaere

Veldhoek

COURTRAI

St Eloi

HILL 60

Hollebeke

Wytschaete

Oostaverne

Menin

R. Lys

Messines

N. Eglise

Comines

St Yves

La Basse Ville

Nieppe

Frelinghien

ARMENTIERES

R. Lys

Bois-Grenier

LILLE

ALLIED LINE
in June 1917

ALLIED LINE
in November 1917

0   5   10

miles

north easterly ridge of German defences which blocked the way to western Belgium, followed by a great cavalry breakthrough, the capture of Ostend and Zeebrugge, and the overthrow of the German armies of the north. Two important objectives were implicit: one, the eviction of the Germans from their Belgian U-boat bases, an aim strongly supported by the Admiralty; and, two, the engagement or neutralization of German reserves until Pétain had rallied the French army.

Not everyone shared Haig's confidence. General Sir Herbert Plumer, who had commanded on the Ypres salient for two years, thought the plan over-ambitious. So did Rawlinson of Somme prominence.

Haig chose a commander with more enthusiasm, Gough, to head the operation. Unlike Plumer, a sixty-year-old infantryman with a reputation for precision, Gough, at forty-seven, had Haig's own cavalry background. That he lacked Plumer's familiarity with the ground was overshadowed in Haig's view by his assurance. If anything, Gough was a greater optimist than his superior. 'We can beat the Germans when and where we like,' he had asserted some weeks earlier.

While Gough plotted the Passchendaele offensive, Plumer was put in charge of a preliminary attack to the south of Ypres, on the so-called Messines Ridge, where the Germans held a wedge in the British line.

For the thoroughness of its preparation, and the sheer weight of explosives expended, the battle of Messines astonished even veteran trench soldiers. Through spring into summer, troops and guns had trundled into Flanders from other British sectors. Towards the end of May, no less than 2,266 artillery pieces, including 756 heavy guns, were concentrated for a sixteen day preparatory bombardment on the eight mile Messines front. An estimated $3\frac{1}{2}$ million shells were fired.

This pulverizing overture was climaxed by the mightiest mine explosions ever seen on the Western Front. Some of the tunnels, an unprecedented three thousand feet and more in length, had been planned as far back as the end of 1915 in anticipation of an assault.

For months, British and dominions miners had wormed their way towards the German positions, fighting underground battles with the enemy, endangered by tunnel collapses, hammered by German *camouflets*. At one period a mechanical borer had been imported. Proven on London's underground railway system, it failed to cope with the Ypresian clay and was abandoned eighty feet beneath the surface.

As the Germans became increasingly aware of the tunnelling their counter-mining had intensified, coupled with bombardments and infantry forays on the shaft areas. Finally, twenty-one mammoth mines were lodged beneath targets spanning the ridge from south of Messines, on the British right, northwards to the villages of Wytschaete and St Eloi. Discounting two, which lay beyond the attack sector, Plumer ordered the remaining nineteen to be detonated simultaneously at zero hour.

The greatest of the mines, a couple of miles south of St Eloi, contained an awesome 95,600 lb of ammonal. Others, of gunpowder and ammonal, were almost as large. On the afternoon of 6 June, the mining officers opened sealed orders to learn that zero hour was 3.10 next morning.

Shortly before 3 o'clock, the British shelling abruptly stopped and

Troops move to the front in horse-drawn wagons through a pulverized village in the Ypres salient.

the Germans, alarmed by the silence, launched clusters of flares above a moonlit No Man's Land. Nine divisions of British, Irish, Australian and New Zealand troops crouched in position for the assault.

Almost 950,000 lb of explosives erupted under the enemy. 'Out of the dark ridges of Messines and Wytschaete gushed enormous volumes of scarlet flame and of earth and smoke all lighted by the flame spilling over into fountains of fierce colour, so that all the countryside was illuminated by red light,' wrote a war correspondent. 'Where some of us stood watching, aghast and spellbound by this burning horror, the ground trembled and surged violently.'

A quarter of a mile from their own mines, detonating officers were hurled across trenches by the blast. The roar of the mines was clearly heard in London, and reputedly at Dublin, five hundred miles from the battle front.

In many places the infantry advanced almost unopposed. Huge black craters gaped before them. Here and there the torn clay bubbled 'like boiling porridge'. Dazed German soldiers were groping blindly about the ridge, some on their hands and knees, some weeping uncontrollably – shattered objects invoking the compassion of their enemy. Ten thousand Germans were listed 'missing' when the day's wounded and dead had been accounted for. A lot would never be traced – their remains were in smithereens.

By 9 a.m. the entire summit of the ridge had been captured.

Though the battle to extend beyond the crest and consolidate was a bloody one, raging for seven days, Messines was a dramatic success by trench war standards. Even so, the war cabinet was hesitant in endorsing the larger Flanders operation until Pétain could substantially co-operate. Haig travelled to London to put his case. The German army, in his view, was near breaking point; 'severe losses' could be avoided. Robertson supported him. On 20 July, the cabinet consented. Eleven days later, the campaign that was to culminate in the horror of Passchendaele went ahead.

Opposite Horse and water-cart flounder in mud at St Eloi. An all-too familiar scene.

After weeks of dry weather rain had begun to fall. This created a dilemma. Between the Ypres salient and the breakthrough point of the northeast ridge, about four and a half miles distant at Passchendaele, the low-lying ground depended critically on a drainage system of dykes and culverts for stability. To shell it meant destroying that system. Not to shell it meant attacking an inviolate enemy.

Haig and Gough refused to forgo the barrage. Among those who warned of the consequences was the senior Tank Corps staff officer, Colonel J. F. C. Fuller:

156

> As we could make no headway against Gough's determination to sink his army in a bottomless bog, we took up the question with GHQ, but with no greater success. We pointed out that ... much of the ground we were to attack over had at one time or another been reclaimed from the sea, and that bombardment would convert it into a bog ... we might just as well have appealed to a brick wall.

Predictably, the tanks stuck fast in the ensuing morass. Half of them were lost in the first battle, while the rest were of very little further use. As Gough's four corps (2nd, 14th, 18th and 19th) of the 5th Army started forward, flanks guarded by part of Plumer's 2nd Army and some French units, German guns contributed to the spreading quagmire. According to plan, the most dangerous enemy batteries should have been taken out by the British guns. In fact, the infantry squelched into a hail of shells.

'It was useless to take any notice where they were falling,' recalled a Lancashire Fusiliers officer. 'They could not be dodged: one had to take one's chance, go forward and leave one's fate to destiny ... fields, trenches, wire, fortifications, roads, ditches and streams were simply churned out of recognition by shell fire. The area was strewn with the mangled remains of men and horses. ... It was hell and slaughter.'

In one important section, German fire disrupted communications so effectively that divisional and corps headquarters received no reliable information on the progress of the battle for five hours.

The German ordnance was well protected, so were the machine guns. Under Ludendorff's direction, these had been disposed in considerable depth on the higher ground in concrete pill-boxes which proved difficult targets. At the same time, the German infantry had been thinned in front to create tactical reserves for prompt counter-strikes. Launched before the British could consolidate, they regained a lot of hard won terrain. On the right, Gough's troops were a mere five hundred yards from the starting line at the end of the first day. At best, progress on the left was about half the hopeful target of four miles.

Two more days of continuous rain saw the battlefield increasingly reverting to its watery origins. Not for nothing had the Belgian farmers of the area been heavily fined if they failed to keep their ditches clear. Now it was hard to find a ditch anywhere amid the profusion of shell holes, glutted like great clay dishes with soupy effluence.

No breakthrough had been achieved, or seemed likely. British casualties, already 31,850, ominously recalled the Somme battles. August brought more rain, torrential on the 8th and 14th. Trenches filled to the brim. Advancing artillery scarcely dared leave the roads, where they still existed. The impossibility of digging-in left the guns exposed.

Before the month was out, casualties had topped sixty-eight thousand, inducing even Gough to doubt the wisdom of continuing. Haig had no doubt. The French army, he noted, was having 'the quiet time desired by General Pétain in which to recover from the Nivelle offensive'. On 21 August, Haig wrote the war cabinet that he was well satisfied.

Nevertheless, he switched responsibility for the main operation from Gough to Plumer, who demanded a pause of three weeks while he reorganized.

In London, an apprehensive government veered more and more

'Stuck fast in the mud'. Picture by Alexander Jamieson, Captain of the 10th York and Lancaster Regiment. His description reads: 'The beginning of an awful experience! One of the 10th Service Battalion York and Lancaster Regiment got held fast by the mud and slime in a shell-hole which flooded as he struggled. To haul him with ropes was impossible as he would have died. It took four nights' hard work by the Pioneers to get him free. His comrade stood by him day and night under fire. He fed him by means of a long stick. When eventually saved both went delirious.'

towards the abandonment of offensive strategy on the Western Front until the Americans took the field in force. Haig maintained his position tenaciously. The pressure in Flanders was preventing Ludendorff from attacking elsewhere. Reluctantly, the cabinet deferred to the commander's views.

In fact, Haig's options were limited. From their elevated positions, the German guns held such an advantage that Plumer and Gough lost more than sixteen thousand men during the September pause. The troops could not be left so exposed through the winter. Short of retreating, Haig had to press on.

The renewed offensive, opened on 20 September, showed promise.

Both in depth and width, Plumer's objectives were more modest than Gough's. His barrages were methodical; strong reserves were deployed to meet the enemy's counter-attack divisions. Moreover, the weather had improved. Within a few days, the white-haired Plumer had won the best part of the Gheluvelt plateau, an important tactical feature, and had beaten off German responses.

Haig's optimism burgeoned. Again, he talked in terms of a breakthrough. 'I pointed out how favourable the situation was and how necessary it was to have all necessary means for exploiting any success.' Neither Plumer nor Gough now thought a breakthrough likely, but they agreed that the Passchendaele ridge might be reached by late October.

The first week of that month damped all but the most ardent hopes. The rain returned. The Germans had reinforced their batteries behind Passchendaele, while the British artillery could barely move in a sea of mud. On 7 October, having completed the capture of the plateau, Plumer and Gough recommended the cessation of the campaign. Haig insisted on going forward.

'We ought to have only one thought now in our minds; namely, *to attack*' – Haig, 11 October.

The resulting battles for Passchendaele were to become legendary for their frightfulness.

If conditions had been bad before, they became appalling. In front of the objective lay a veritable swamp several miles across. Mobility was minimal. Infantry units took five hours to 'march' a mile; supplies and ammunition moved more slowly, barely distinguishable beneath the oozing slime which smothered them; a dozen or more men might be needed to heave a stretcher case through the stinking mud.

Under fire the horror became complete. Descriptions of the fighting evoke immense sadness:

Opposite Shell-shocked and shell-torn, the living huddle with the dead at Broodseinde Ridge, 1917.

161

'We fell into mud and writhed out like wasps crawling from rotten plums. ... The dead and wounded were piled on each other's backs. ... The second wave, coming up behind, were knocked over in their tracks and lay in heaving mounds ...' Those unable to crawl into the slopping shell holes were doomed. 'They had to lie where they were until a stray bullet found them or they were blown to pieces. Their heartrending cries pierced the incessant din of explosions.'

Pitifully the wounded tried to mark their places by sticking their rifles upright in the drenched earth. 'There was a forest of rifles, until they were uprooted by shell bursts or knocked down like skittles by bullets.' Such stretcher-bearers as survived floundered in a nightmare of anguish and frustration.

Through October to November the troops struggled to keep moving. Sheer bloody-minded bravery kept many going, but the futility of the sacrifice was telling. An infantry subaltern had 'never seen men so broken and demoralized' as the survivors of one company butchered in the advance.

The next day, we were ordered to retake the line, and then our units sank to the lowest pitch of which I have ever been cognizant. It looked hopeless – the men were so utterly done. However, the attempt had to be made, and we moved up that night ... the fellows were dropping out unconscious along the road. They have guts! That's the only way to express it. We found the line not advanced but some thirty yards behind where we had left it ... thick with dead and wounded. Some of the Manchesters were there yet, seven days wounded and not tended.

By 6 November, when the Canadians finally stumbled into Passchendaele, it was too late in all respects to exploit the achievement. On the 10th, Haig called off the offensive.

Since its commencement on 31 July, an advance of about five miles had been paid for by 244,897 British casualties, 100,000 of them after Haig's insistence on continuing in October. The German losses, undisclosed, were undoubtedly terrible – possibly approaching those of the British – but Haig's purpose of absorbing the enemy's reserves had not been realized. Despite the fighting in Flanders, Germany had moved a reserve army to defeat the Italians at Caporetto.

Opposite Passchendaele landscape with water-filled shell-holes.

Statistically, the Ypres offensive of 1917 was marginally less costly than the 1916 Somme attack. Morally, it was more destructive, for the fact that so little had been learned from the earlier tragedy struck countless men as inexcusable. Beneath the grim November sky of Flanders British forces were as disillusioned by Passchendaele as the French were by Nivelle.

Chapter 9

Cambrai

British casualties on the Western Front approached two million after Passchendaele, more than a third dead. As in the Somme battles, when the majority of Kitchener's 1914 recruits had discovered the full horror and chaos of the battlefield for the first time, a fresh vintage of soldiery had lost its zest in Flanders. Once eager and trusting, the trench warrior grew resentful and cynical.

For some, it was primarily methods that were questionable.

A young infantry officer, Basil Liddell Hart, later an authority of wide repute, exemplified scepticism centred on martial competence. '"Theirs not to reason why; theirs but to do and die" had become a habit. ... I wanted to know "the reason why" in order to teach and train the men under me. And the more I studied the question, the clearer it became that there was little or no reason in the methods we were pursuing.'

Others had deeper doubts. While public men persisted in the lofty platitudes of 1914, the trench soldier saw the war less and less in an idealistic light, more and more as a form of mass murder in the interest of people in little danger. In many cases vexation aroused by staff officers in the rear was overshadowed by bitterness towards the 'people at home', the political and industrial mandarins.

Newspapers and public speakers, glorifying the fighting, contributed to the ordinary soldier's feeling that he was being not only lied to but lied about. Resentment was exacerbated by the comparatively mild effect of the war on conditions in Britain, where employment was high and the prosperity of many all too evident.

Writer and academic Vivian de Sola Pinto, home on sick leave at the end of 1917, noted the disturbing contrast between the hell of the trenches and the complacent life style of his middle class well-wishers in England:

> As I gulped down their champagne with a fatuous smile on my face I felt horribly unreal, a sort of ghost from another world, the real world of the brotherhood of the front line. And when we went to the theatre to see *Chu Chin Chow* and *The Bing Boys*, as I looked at the crowded auditorium and the glittering lights I could not help wondering whether it would not perhaps be a good thing if a tank should come lurching through the stalls to jolt all those well fed people out of their complacency.

More than ever after Passchendaele, the trench soldier felt isolated from his homeland, an anonymous 'nobody' struggling for survival in a wholesale killing process which made the motives for fighting seem increasingly irrelevant. The pals' battalions were

Opposite British soldiers hear Mass amid debris in Cambrai Cathedral, 1918.

Stretcher bearers attend
wounded soldier during
battle near Potijze,
1917.

tattered. Men had watched their chums struck dead or carried away bleeding on stretchers. Those who remained clung together with fierce loyalty, each propping the other's flagging spirits.

Several factors prevented the decline in morale assuming the proportions manifested in the French mutinies.

One was the pronounced emphasis on discipline in the British army. To the average soldier, discipline simply meant the unquestioning obedience to any senior rank, a quality ingrained from the first in all recruits. 'Orders is orders,' was the saying. (Interestingly, the identical sentiment, '*befehl ist befehl*', was a common phrase in the highly disciplined German army.) Since most of the men, reared in an age when nonconformity was unfashionable, accepted the system, few fell seriously foul of it.

Those who did faced swift and often rugged sanctions. Acts of indiscipline classified as cowardice in action, desertion or mutiny, were punishable during the war by the death sentence, officially applied in rather more than three hundred cases in the British army.

166

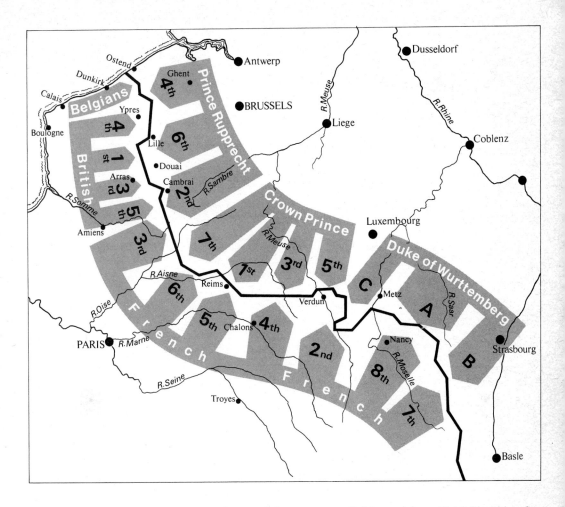

Map 6 Disposition of Armies, Western Front, end of 1917.

A more frequent sentence for serious misdemeanour, field punishment, carried the liability of being detained in chains and, for periods, bound to a fixed object – the procedure known to soldiers as 'crucifixion'.

Summary justice of a less drastic nature (sometimes 'informal' as in the classic case of men being obliged to stand in water-filled shell holes) was subject to few legalistic niceties. On the whole, routine charges were dealt with on the basis of upholding the authority of the n.c.o.s who brought them rather than with any fine regard for the rights of the men charged. Most soldiers accepted fairly phlegmatically the premise that in effect they had no rights and that an awkward n.c.o. could ensure a stiff sentence for any man if he wished.

But if imposed discipline provided a scaffolding of support when morale slumped, a more important factor was the peculiar self-

167

discipline of the British soldier, summarized by one observer as 'a sort of bloody-minded refusal to dodge the slings of outrageous fortune'. In extremes of adversity it provided a reserve of endurance which sometimes astonished the men themselves.

Another element of adhesion to common purpose was the care and responsibility displayed by a large proportion of officers and n.c.o.s towards the other ranks. While Haig considered it unnecessary to visit the Passchendaele front and see conditions for himself, few regimental officers held back from the foremost posts, nor spared themselves in alleviating the suffering of their troops where it was possible to do so.

Finally, impelled to the brink of despondency by generals content, as Churchill put it, 'to fight machine-gun bullets with the breasts of gallant men', the British army in Europe was shaken from despair by a new and unexpected action – a battle so novel in its early stages that it seemed at last to have unlocked the stalemate of three years and released the trench soldier from his wretched hole.

On 20 November 1917, the 3rd Army launched the battle of Cambrai.

Convinced from the first of the futility of using tanks in the swamps of Flanders, Fuller and his immediate superior, a lanky brigadier named Hugh Elles who commanded the Tank Corps in France, had been scanning the front for a more fitting battlefield. The area they hit on was in the 3rd Army sector before the prosperous weaving town of Cambrai, where the rolling downs were still relatively green and firm.

Both Elles and Fuller were young men in their thirties, impatient to see their machines employed to best advantage. So far life had been fraught with obstructions. The CIGS regarded tanks as a 'somewhat desperate innovation'. Many generals voiced a ruder antipathy. The War Office attached so little importance to the new weapon that in August it had actually proposed a scheme to make good some of the losses in Flanders by drafting tank crews to the infantry.

Haig had been more encouraging. His order for a thousand vehicles during the Somme fighting had raised the hopes of tank commanders. But he had done little to chase up production, and had used such tanks as he possessed uninspiredly.

The Tank Corps still awaited the implementation of what it considered its most apt role: surprise attack in mass on favourable

168

territory. Interest in Cambrai coincided with discussions in the 3rd Army, now under General Sir Julian Byng, concerning a possible attack in the region to relieve pressure in Flanders. Byng, like Elles, was interested in a surprise assault, for the Hindenburg line at that point was lightly manned and might be overrun before German reserves arrived.

Since the attainment of surprise ruled out using artillery to destroy hostile defensive works in advance, Byng was sympathetic towards using tanks on a large scale to smash through barbed wire and trenches ahead of his infantry.

At first Haig was cool. His hopes then were still high for Flanders, and reserves could not be spared for a new move. October brought a change of heart. Now the northern blow was faltering, morale sinking. Criticism from Britain had begun to bite. Haig was ready to take a risk to get quick results.

Map 7 Battle of Cambrai (British 3rd Army).

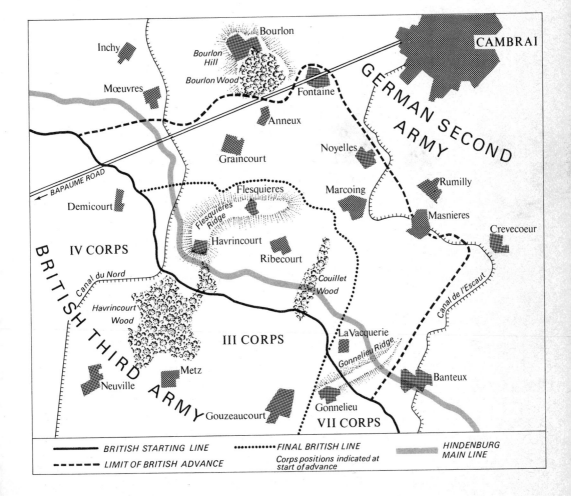

BRITISH STARTING LINE

LIMIT OF BRITISH ADVANCE

FINAL BRITISH LINE

Corps positions indicated at start of advance

HINDENBURG MAIN LINE

On 13 October, approval was given for the so-called 'secret operation' to take place in November. Byng's aim was to overrun the German defences on a six mile front, capture the two main features in the area, the ridges of Flesquiers and Bourlon, then pass cavalry between them to liberate Cambrai, about seven miles behind the German line. From Cambrai, the attack would drive northeast towards Valenciennes, rolling up the German front.

For this purpose, Byng depended on six infantry divisions, with a further two in support and three in reserve; five cavalry divisions; and three tank brigades – plus field artillery. It was a modest force for so ambitious a project, and the Tank Corps leaders, though eager to prove themselves, were apprehensive of its scope. Their own hopes had inclined towards a heavy raid rather than a full scale offensive.

That Haig himself was conscious of his low reserves and the lateness of the season was evident in a proviso he attached to the proposals. If the position after forty-eight hours was not promising, he would call the operation off.

The Tank Corps prepared excitedly. Of 474 Mark IV vehicles allocated for the attack, 376 were fighting tanks, the remainder equipped for supply, communications or wire clearing duties. One problem they faced was the exceptional size of the Hindenburg trenches. Each tank was to carry a huge fascine of brushwood on its nose to drop into the obstacle, thus providing its own bridge. The fascines, bound with chains, weighed nearly two tons apiece.

The drill was simple. Every third tank was to drop a fascine in the first trench line, two more vehicles crossing by the same bridge to place their own fascines in the second and third trenches. In this manner, the tanks would penetrate the full depth of the defensive system, shooting up its occupants and crushing the wire for the following infantry. Other machines, fitted with grappling gear, would drag the wire clear ahead of the cavalry.

Strict secrecy surrounded forward movements as the day of assault approached. Tanks inched towards the front by night, their engines throttled back to a low rumble. White tapes had been laid as guides. Where these had been ripped up by the churning tracks, commanders walked immediately ahead of their machines, signalling with glowing cigarettes.

Security was maintained successfully. On 16 November, four days from the offensive, the commander of the German 2nd Army on the sector, General von der Marwitz, reported, 'Major attacks of the enemy against the front of the 2nd Army are not to be expected in the foreseeable future.'

On the eve of the assault, Elles announced his intention of personally leading the first major tank operation in martial history. Next morning, as the crews climbed aboard, Elles squeezed into a machine named 'Hilda' and reappeared through the manhole on top with the corps flag. At 6.10 a.m., the drivers opened their throttles. The armour lurched forward through the dawn mists.

There was no sound from the enemy.

'It seemed almost too good to be true, this steady rumbling forward over marvellous going; no craters, no shelling,' declared a tank crew member. 'Emerging out of the gloom a dark mass came steadily towards us – the German wire. It appeared absolutely impenetrable ... but it squashed flat as we moved on, and remained flat.'

Reaching the German trenches, 'female' tanks swung along the parapets, machine-gunning dismayed Germans as they emerged from their dug-outs, while other vehicles dropped their fascines and crashed on. 'Down the whole line tanks were dipping and rearing up and clawing their way across into the almost unravaged country beyond.'

Immediately behind, dogging the tanks in platoon files, came the men of Byng's two infantry corps, the 3rd and 4th, to carry the confused trenches and dug-outs at bayonet point. Those following the leaders found the notorious Hindenburg line an open cave of German corpses and treasure: pots of coffee and soup still simmering, bottles of claret in the officers' quarters, expensive field glasses, and many other items waiting to be picked up.

An officer of the 51st Highland Division was greeted by a Scots sergeant smoking a long cigar. 'All his men were smoking cigars, and it was difficult to find a Highlander that morning without one.'

So swift and complete was the fall of the German line that staff officers on both sides found the news unbelievable. Indeed, time spent verifying a seemingly impossible achievement significantly delayed the dispatch of the British cavalry. Ludendorff, informed of the operation soon after 8 a.m., immediately ordered a counterattack; but the few German reserves close to the front could not stem the advance, let alone push the British back. Before midday, Marwitz was preparing a wholesale withdrawal in the area.

It was an extraordinary day. As the tanks regrouped to renew their charge, British field artillery could be seen actually galloping forward to take up new positions. Suddenly the gods of war seemed to have donned traditional panoply. Soon, it was expected, the cavalry would surge through towards Cambrai, where already rumours of liberation were stirring.

By evening German prisoners could be counted in thousands. A larger number quantified their dead or wounded comrades. Two divisions of the 2nd Army were in shreds; scores of field and machine guns captured. In a few hours Byng's troops had advanced three or four miles on a front of six miles against the strongest defence system on the Western Front. By trench war standards their own casualties, rather more than four thousand, were uniquely low.

The news transported Britain. Church bells were rung, congratulations speeded to the fighting troops. Wrote Churchill later:

> Accusing as I do without exception all the great Allied (*sic*) offensives of 1915, 1916 and 1917 as needless and wrongly conceived operations of infinite cost, I am bound to reply to the question – what else could be done? I answer it, pointing to the battle of Cambrai, 'this could have been done'. This in many variants, in larger and better forms, ought to have been done.

The ultimate sentence was the crucial one, for while the first real demonstrations of tank power heralded a revolution of military techniques which would soon render trench warfare obsolete, the battle of Cambrai itself was to end in bitter disappointment.

Byng's tanks were still too few, their development too primitive, the generals insufficiently perceptive of their needs and capabilities, for the triumph to continue. Vainly, Elles and Fuller had asked that a reserve of machines should be held back for exploitation of the first success. When the tank brigades rallied at the end of the initial day, 179 of the fighting vehicles were out of action, most through mechanical troubles or ditching, and the rest had been in action for sixteen hours.

With no reserves, exhausted crews and vehicles needing maintenance services had to be prepared for immediate re-employment. It was afternoon before they reached the forward positions the next day.

Everywhere, delay and hesitation eroded the advantage of the early hours. Three years of immobility, interspersed with unimaginative and impersonal mass attacks, had deprived commanders of the capacity for bold, spontaneous decisions. For the first time since autumn 1914 the dream of the generals, a war of dashing movement, had been within grasp. But the dream was based on an extinct force, a ghost army of pre-war vintage whose talent for flexibility lay buried in the trenches.

Even the cavalry, with its tradition of reckless intrepidity, had grown circumspect:

'We met the vanguard of the cavalry at the village of Ribecourt, a place that had been in our hands since 7 o'clock that morning,'

'Over the top'. Painting
by John Nash.

'Gassed'. Painting by
J. S. Sargent.

Above Lt John Cridland Barrett leading an attack on an enemy trench which earned him the VC. Painting by Terence Cuneo.

Remembrance

Right Remembrance card in silk.

reported a tank officer. 'Now, four hours later, the cavalry was advancing as cautiously as if Germans might be expected round every corner. ... It was all too late. The mounted squadrons were only just crossing No Man's Land and it was nearly 2 p.m., just six hours after the barbed wire had been cleared for them.'

Derelict Mark IV tank on Ypres battlefield, 1917.

Time and again, after the initial surge, opportunities for exploitation passed while orders were awaited from the distant rear. In some cases instructions arrived so slowly that the enemy had re-occupied previously vacated positions before the troops advanced.

As the moment approached for Haig's forty-eight hour reappraisal Flesquiers Ridge was in British hands; but the vital Bourlon Ridge to the north, overlooking the western approaches to Cambrai, was still held by the enemy. The 3rd Corps to the right of Flesquiers had stopped advancing and stood on the defensive. Several German divisions had arrived in the area from the Aisne and Flanders, and other enemy reinforcements were on the way.

The arguments for withdrawal to an organized line were powerful, but the nearness of Cambrai and the jubilation which had greeted the breakthrough were strong inducements to sustain the offensive.

Haig opted for the latter course though content for the 3rd Corps to hold its ground. On 23 November, the 4th Corps was thrown against Bourlon Ridge. It had begun to snow. A few tanks were available for use against the two main objectives, the village of Bourlon and Bourlon Wood, but co-ordination between infantry and armour was breaking down.

At the village the tanks arrived before the infantry and were obliged to retire with losses. Without close support from foot troops the slow-moving vehicles were vulnerable to bold action by enemy bombers, who hurled bundles of grenades at the driving tracks, and to field artillery operating at point-blank range. One German officer, standing by his gun to the very end, knocked out five tanks single-handed at Cambrai – a performance which earned him the unusual distinction of being mentioned in Haig's despatches.

At Bourlon Wood, on the summit of the ridge, it was the tanks that arrived late, due to lack of fuel and ammunition. Welsh troops took the wood in vicious fighting, but it quickly became the target of determined counter-attacks and bombardment with high explosive and gas shells.

In July the Germans had used the first shells filled with mustard gas, dichlorethyl sulphide. The substance caused dangerous burns, sometimes resulting in death or blindness, and took a heavy toll among the unsuspecting troops. Between three and four thousand cases of contamination were treated after one bombardment. Though the British army had promptly ordered mustard gas for its own use, supplies were not to become available until almost the war's end.

By 26 November the surviving tanks with the 4th Corps had been withdrawn for re-fitting, and the struggle for the ridge continued without tank support. The same day, Crown Prince Rupprecht of Bavaria, commanding the northern group of German armies, decided that reinforcements in the sector were adequate to launch a major counter-stroke. His plan was to attack the two flanks of the salient won by the British, recapture the Hindenburg positions and cut off Byng's force.

'Never has there been such an opportunity,' agreed Ludendorff.

Twenty German divisions now faced nineteen British, discounting cavalry. They struck on the 30th. Byng was caught unprepared. Despite reports from the front of German massing, no instructions had been issued by his staff, the tanks had not been recalled, there were few reserves.

In the north the Germans were parried, but the British line in the south broke after violent fighting and a confused retreat ensued, many of the retiring troops starved of ammunition. 'We were on undulating country, devoid of cover, ammunition gone, completely exhausted and under-nourished,' wrote one fugitive. 'On our heels were two fresh divisions of German troops.'

Byng's position was desperate. Dismounted cavalry, pushed in as infantry, fought bravely. In the south, the Germans re-took part of the Hindenburg line. 'Every traverse was contested,' witnessed a German storm troop officer. 'Mills bombs and stick bombs crossed and recrossed. Behind each corner we found dead or still quivering bodies.' Ultimately disaster was averted by a superb counterattack by the Guards Division, one of Byng's reserves, and the reappearance of a tank brigade.

The Tank Corps had been clearing camp and entraining its battered vehicles in the rear when news of the German advance arrived. Fuller was unsure whether it was 'a joke or an actual fact'. A cabled SOS put him out of doubt. Every tank that could be salvaged in an approximation of fighting order was assembled and ordered forward. There were sixty-three. For the next two days, they fought without pause.

'They accomplished,' Fuller observed later, 'what I have always felt to be one of the most remarkable tank achievements of the war.'

By 3 December, both sides were spent. While the Germans

XI Corps entering Lille, 1918.

A Mark V tank going into action. Painting by Bernard Adeney.

prepared to consolidate the British executed an orderly withdrawal to tenable ground. After thirteen days of fighting, the Cambrai offensive ended with the 3rd Army retaining much of the territory won on the first day while the Germans gained a strip almost as large to the south of it. Troop losses were about equal, probably exceeding fifty thousand in each case, including prisoners.

Less than a third of the tanks engaged were recovered, and those in poor shape. Few saw any further action, for by next year the Mark IV would be replaced by the more advanced Mark V, faster and capable of being driven and steered by one man.

Indeed, the stimulus given to tank production was the most positive result of the whole affair.

The upsetting conclusion to Cambrai brought recrimination on many heads. Byng placed the blame on his troops, or more precisely their rawness and inadequate training. The regimental officers, on the other hand, were more inclined to find culprits among the generals. Haig, by no means blameless in some eyes, appeared to take both sides, accepting Byng's view while soon afterwards replacing two of the corps commanders.

Disagreement was rife in many quarters at the year's end. The ghastly slaughter of the 1917 offensives, to no decisive advantage, produced an increasingly articulate British lobby for a peace based on compromise. The Labour movement was talking internationally to the same end. Lord Lansdowne, a former cabinet minister, published a letter in the press suggesting assurances to Germany that her ruin as a great power was not the aim of the allies, and that Britain was willing to consider some sort of pact.

But compromise was anathema to the military leaders. Haig and Robertson insisted that the enemy was weakening and would break if Britain kept the pressure on. Hindenburg and Ludendorff, too, were convinced they could seize victory if their government remained firm. In Britain, and in France (where Georges Clemenceau – known as the Tiger for his hot temper – had emerged from political crisis as prime minister), the heads of government had not abandoned hope of a military solution, though Lloyd George more than ever deprecated Haig's strategy.

Again, the British premier saw a means of diminishing Haig's influence and devising fresh policies through a closer strategic association with Britain's allies. On 1 December, a new supreme allied war council met to consider plans for 1918. Haig, already intent on yet another great British offensive, bitterly agreed with Robertson on 'the impossibility of working with such a man' as Lloyd George.

The squabbling was abruptly drowned on 3 December by an armistice between Bolshevik Russia and Germany. Placing the initiative clearly in the German camp, it damped Haig's plans with conspicuous rapidity. 'We must be prepared to meet a strong and sustained hostile offensive,' he asserted the same day. 'It is therefore of the first importance that Army commanders give their urgent and personal attention to the organization of zones for defensive purposes.'

Chapter 10

The Return of Movement

Germany entered 1918 buoyed by the collapse of Russia – and to a lesser extent the collapse of Rumania, which had taken the allied side – but with time against her. The U-boat war had failed in its objectives, whereas the allied blockade was proving increasingly effective. Food was short in Germany. Her accomplices, Turkey, Bulgaria and Austria-Hungary, were weakening. Before long the build-up of American troops in France would tip the scales irrevocably and fatally.

Ludendorff had to exploit his immediate initiative decisively. With some two hundred divisions now at his disposal, he proposed an all-out attempt to break the western stalemate in early spring, crushing free France and routing the British on the continent.

The mighty offensive he launched in March marked the end of the trench war as characterized by deadlock, and revived a war of stormy movement. There would still be trenches, old ones and some new ones, but the great campaigns of 1918 raged over and beyond them with a fluidity not seen since Moltke's armies raced for Paris. In a single week parts of the front shifted forty miles. As a veteran soldier put it at the time, 'The whole bloody war has changed.'

Ludendorff based his methods on a study of both western and eastern experience. In contemplating the failure of western offensives for three years, he started afresh from the proposition that the pursuit of strategic aims was futile unless tactical success was possible. 'Tactics had to be considered before purely strategic objects.' Surprise, he concluded, was the first tactical necessity, hence the massing of assault troops should be concealed and bombardments delayed until the last minute, when gas shells should be used to stun the enemy.

More novel to the West were the infiltration tactics he borrowed from the Russian front. Dispensing with the notion of set piece attacks by infantry with closely briefed objectives, Ludendorff proposed a probing technique in which machine-gun scouts were thrown forward to seek weaknesses in the opposing line. Pistol lights then directed the main bodies of infantry to the weak points.

Opposite Ever-ready but seldom used – British cavalry (Scots Greys) resting near Montreuil, 1918.

Similarly, on a wider scale, the selection of offensive sectors was governed primarily by the enemy's vulnerability. Having achieved a breakthrough on the line of least tactical resistance, strategic possibilities could be assessed and seized accordingly. It was a policy of calculated opportunism, and it began brilliantly.

The first blow fell on 21 March, against the armies of Byng and Gough. After a violent bombardment with high explosive and gas, sixty-two divisions of the German 2nd, 17th and 18th Armies

advanced on a forty-seven mile front astride the Somme valley from Arras, through St Quentin to La Fère. Twenty-six British divisions opposed them in eerie conditions. A thick mist, reducing visibility to less than a dozen yards at sunrise, persisted most of the morning.

For many defenders, sight was further impaired by the need to wear gas masks, and by smoke bombs put down by the Germans. British artillery support was severely hampered.

In the north Byng held Arras, but south of the Somme the

German probes sniffed out the thinner defences on Gough's sector and the grey divisions of the Kaiser's 18th Army crashed through. The swift penetration of scouting groups, especially through woods and valleys, confused an inflexible defensive system.

'This scientific method of infiltration made the defenders think all the time that their flanks were being turned,' wrote the war correspondent Neville Lytton. 'Corps and divisional headquarters moved too rapidly to the rear ... the sense of being abandoned was an awful thing for a regiment.'

British dead in front of wrecked tank during the German offensive, 1918.

185

Before the unequal weight and unaccustomed methods of the onslaught, the right of Gough's army swung back like a fractured gate, opening vistas of Compiègne and Paris. German spirits soared. Like the French before Nivelle's offensive, Ludendorff's troops had been prepared by stirring promises of victory. Now, that long elusive prospect seemed within grasp at last.

'For the first time after years of weary defence in the waste of the trenches,' declared Crown Prince William, commander of the advancing army group, 'the hour of liberation had struck and the command had gone forth to Germany's sons to strike for final victory in the open field. As if shaking off some horrible nightmare, my infantry had risen from the trenches and, crushing all resistance with unexampled vigour, had broken through.'

For a week, Gough's men retreated with monotonous regularity, while the French on their right struggled to keep contact, to plug the gap. On 27 March, the enemy took Montdidier, ominously near Paris, cutting the railway to the capital. Further north, the British were falling back on Amiens. Ahead of the German tide, an

Saints and other ranks. Troops help salvage treasures from damaged church, Armentières, 1918.

elaborate allied communications system geared to static trench warfare was in confusion.

In this desperate situation, Haig removed Gough, placed Rawlinson in command of the 5th Army, and acceded to the appointment of Foch, the least pessimistic of the allied generals, as supreme chief of the forces in France and Belgium.

Meanwhile, Ludendorff had made his first mistake. The principle of pursuing the line of least resistance urged an immediate concentration of his reserves on the southern breakthrough. Instead, perhaps startled by its very swiftness, he reined in the galloping 18th Army while persisting in a futile assault on the northern bastion of Arras. By the time he shifted the weight of his forces south, the crucial moment had passed. Ludendorff had sold short his own policy.

For two days at the end of March, the 18th Army obeyed orders and marked time. When it resumed its attack on the 30th, French reserves were streaming into the breach by truck, on horseback, even on bicycles, and the 5th Army had rallied. The Germans could make little progress.

Ten days later Ludendorff opened a secondary offensive against the southern flank of the Ypres salient. Again he found a weak point. Two Portuguese divisions fighting with the British were routed, and what the German commander had planned as a diversion flared into a major drive for the Channel ports. Raging for three weeks, the so-called 'battle of Lys' carried the divisions of Prince Rupprecht ten miles towards their objectives and cost the British 1st and 2nd Armies more than 300,000 casualties. Then Ludendorff called a halt for fear of a counter-stroke.

His next major blow was planned for Flanders. Before it could take place, however, another diversionary offensive exploded into a full-scale issue. On 27 May, fifteen divisions of Prince William's command fell on two French divisions in the Chemin des Dames region between Reims and Soissons. Completely unexpected, the attack carried thirteen miles on the first day, drawing heavy reserves from both sides, and reached the Marne before losing impetus.

The Germans claimed the capture of 50,000 prisoners, 600 guns and 2,000 machine guns.

The French were very near despair. As their harassed forces marched and counter-marched the country in response to one crisis after another, Pétain joined the ranks of gloom. Only Foch preserved an aura of confidence. The British had been cruelly mauled. Divisions hastily recalled from active service in Italy, 187

Map 8 Western Front,
July–November 1918.

Salonica and Palestine, plus fresh drafts from England, less than
replaced their casualties. Ten divisions had to be broken up. Haig's
offensive plans for spring had vanished.

Not once, but several times, as Lloyd George observed later, 'the
Germans in a few days had broken through the allied line to a depth
which the British and French offensives had never reached after
weeks and months of laborious and costly effort. The prisoners and
guns captured by the enemy in each of these battles exceeded the
highest record of the allies in any of their great offensives.'

But Ludendorff's attainments were marred by one omission. His
tactical triumphs had failed to produce a strategic master-stroke.
The chinks had been found in the allied armour; the knife had gone
in deep and repeatedly. Yet no vital organ had been struck. By the
end of spring, he had committed too many reserves to launch an
all out summer campaign without a pause to rest and regroup his
troops. The pause proved fatal to German hopes.

The turn in Ludendorff's fortunes was presaged at Chateau-
Thierry, a symbolic action in the May offensive. For at Chateau-

Thierry the German tide was stemmed by Americans.

Led by the determined General John Pershing, whose humble
origins contrasted sharply with those of most allied generals, the
first 'doughboys' in France had caused amusement by their easy-
going attitudes. Chateau-Thierry, earning them the respect of both
friends and the enemy, served plain notice of a dynamic new current
running against Germany. From the end of April, American troops
arrived at the rate of 300,000 a month to emphasize the message.

Ludendorff's troops had made their best efforts. In June, and
again in mid-July, they tried unsuccessfully to pinch out the tongues
of allied territory between the wedges left by the German advance.
Stuck on an indented front, the German armies were increasingly
at risk from counter-attacks from a recuperating enemy.

The first came on 18 July.

Foch had waited grimly since April to seize the initiative. Now
he meant to keep it to the very end. Led by a swarm of new light
tanks, French troops, directed by Pétain and supported by British
and American divisions, slammed into the north east flank of the 189

THE WONDER WEEK OF NOVEMBER, 1918
The Crash of Kaiserdom.

"The abdication of William II. and his son is an event so momentous that its symbolic importance cannot be overstated. The Hohenzollern Monarchy was in Europe the very keystone of the arch of militarist autocracy. For half a century it bestrode the earth like a veritable Colossus."—"The Daily Chronicle," November 11.

The ex-King Ludwig III. of Bavaria

It is reported that a republic has been proclaimed in Bavaria and the reigning house deposed. The ex-King Ludwig III. succeeded his cousin, the mad King Otto, in 1913; he married the Archduchess Marie Thérésa of Austria-Este, and his heir was the Crown Prince Rupprecht, commander of a group of German armies

The ex-German Crown Prince

Friedrich Wilhelm, Crown Prince of the German Empire and of Prussia, was born in 1882, and married Princess Cecilie, daughter of the late Friedrich Franz III. of Mecklenburg-Schwerin. He has resigned his succession to the throne, and at present nothing certain is known of his late

The ex-King Wilhelm II. of Wurttemberg

Wilhelm II. was the son of the late Prince Friedrich of Wurttemberg (cousin of the late King Karl I.), and ascended the throne on October 6, 1891, on the death of Karl I. A republic has been proclaimed in the kingdom, and Wilhelm II. has fled from his capital

The ex-Duke of Brunswick

The abdication of Ernest Augustus, Duke of Brunswick, is announced. He was born on November 7, 1887, and was the son of Ernest Augustus, Duke of Cumberland. In 1913 he married the Princess Victoria Louisa, only daughter of the ex-Emperor Wilhelm II.

The ex-Grand Duke of Hesse

A republic has been proclaimed in the Grand Duchy of Hesse-Darmstadt. The ex-Grand Duke Ernst Ludwig was born in 1868, the son of Grand Duke Ludwig IV. and Princess Alice of England. He succeeded to the throne in 1892. He has two sons

The ex-Grand Duke of Oldenburg

The Grand Duke Friedrich August has been dethroned. He succeeded his father, the Grand Duke Peter, in 1900. He was twice married, and has one son and three daughters, the eldest of whom, Princess Sophia, married Prince Eitel Friedrich of Prussia

Marne salient from the woods of Villers-Cotterets. At the same time the allied air forces, including Americans, dived in unprecedented numbers on the German lines, shooting up troops and destroying bridges in the rear.

Stubbornly, the Germans held the gates of the salient open long enough for their threatened groups to escape.

Ludendorff had barely extricated his forces from the Marne when, on 8 August, Rawlinson struck from Amiens to avenge the battered 5th Army, now reinforced and designated the 4th Army. Secrecy, the new offensive imperative, had been the keynote of his preparations. Every officer and man had the notice 'Keep Your Mouth Shut' pasted in his small book; paved roads were sanded to minimize traffic noise; civilians were prevented from entering the build-up zone.

So complete was the surprise that divisional staffs of Prince Rupprecht's armies were overrun in their headquarters by the leading British tanks. Rather more machines were used than at Cambrai. The Germans had not bothered to entrench themselves. South of the Somme they were literally swept aside by Australian and Canadian troops who, operating beside the French 1st Army, did not stop until they reached the wastes of the 1916 battlefields.

'The British assault troops behind the tanks surged from all directions,' witnessed a German gunner. 'Machine guns rattled; bullets sped around us. We dashed from hole to hole. Some of our survivors strayed too far to the right and were captured. Others, whom we had believed dead, turned up after two days.'

The Germans admitted twenty-eight thousand losses on the first day. The number of prisoners taken alone exceeded Rawlinson's casualties.

Later known as the battle of Amiens, the action convinced Ludendorff that his plans had failed. '8 August was the black day of the German army ... the worst day I ever went through,' he wrote. 'We had to resign ourselves now to a continuation of the enemy's offensive. Their success had been too easy. Their wireless was jubilant, announcing with truth that the morale of the German army was no longer what it had been.'

At Spa, the German crown council concluded that, 'We can no longer hope to break the war will of our enemies by military operations.'

Rawlinson's offensive was followed by a flurry of allied punches as Foch piled the pressure on a gloomy foe. On 10 August, the French 3rd Army struck to the right of the British, followed by the French 10th Army further south. On 21 August, the British 3rd

Opposite 'The Wonder Week of November, 1918.' The fall of the Hohenzollern Monarchy.

Army pounced, then, on the 26th, the British 1st Army. A few days later, Pershing's Americans waded into the southerly German salient of St Mihiel. The first big independent attack mounted by the US forces, it proved highly successful.

Now more than a million strong, the American 1st Army pressed into the heavily defended Argonne with what the German commander in the south described as 'savage determination'.

Allied casualties were not light. The British lost 189,000 men between 8 August and 26 September, a large proportion of them youths of eighteen and nineteen. But the figures were dramatically lower than expected for comparable gains a year earlier.

Demoralization in the German ranks was accelerating rapidly. Crown Prince William issued a special order denouncing pacifist propaganda and incipient mutiny in his armies. Throughout the German nation, demands for peace and food were rising week by week. While Foch planned an all-out autumn bid for victory, Ludendorff was reduced to holding on in the hope of a favourable armistice.

The last act opened at the end of September with a grand allied assault through the length of the German line. On the St Quentin-Cambrai front, the forty-one divisions of Haig's armies opened a breach six miles deep in the enemy's defences. To the north, Belgian and allied forces under the personal command of King Albert of Belgium surged forward to end the long and bleak occupation of that country. In the south, French and American armies drove the Argonne and Meuse towards Mezières.

Almost simultaneously, news broke that Germany's Balkan ally, Bulgaria, had collapsed before an allied attack from Salonica.

On 29 September, Hindenburg informed a council of war that 'the situation demanded an immediate armistice to save a catastrophe'. Negotiations and fighting dragged on until November, when, on the morning of the 11th, British units finally received the message: 'Hostilities will cease at 11 hours today. ... Troops will stand fast on the line reached at that hour. ... There will be no intercourse of any description with the enemy until receipt of orders from GHQ.'

Foch's last order of the day to allied troops contained the words, 'You have won the greatest battle in History.' For the most part, they were glad to be done with it. In the British lines the mood was less of jubilation than dazed relief.

A million British and dominions combatants had not lived to see the end. A further 2,289,860 had been wounded in the holocaust. (Final figures for killed and wounded of other nations were: Russia 9,150,000; France 6,160,800; Italy 2,197,000; USA 350,300.) Of all types and theatres of operation, the trench war of the Western Front had claimed by far the heaviest toll of British manhood, a fact coloured by the harsh irony that the armies of both sides had first taken to trenches to save losses.

Recriminations abounded. But the more profound implications of the war soon overtook them. Within two decades the condemnation of military leaders, overshadowed by economic depression and the condemnation of political leaders, had given way to preparations for another war. In 1939, the sons of the trench soldiers enlisted to re-contest the old battlefields. The new war lasted longer, ranged wider, placed civilians in greater jeopardy than the 1914-18 war.

Yet Britain's military casualties were only half as many. The day of the trench war was over.

Select Bibliography

The *History of the Great War: Military Operations* by the Committee of Imperial Defence (various volumes, London, since 1932) has been used as the general arbiter of events, and all figures for British casualties are based on official records. It is sometimes charged that these underestimate the losses. Among works summarizing the years of conflict, two may be recommended for their contrasting views on the military leadership. *Sir Douglas Haig's Command 1915–1918* by G. A. B. Dewer, assisted by Lt-Col. J. H. Boaston (2 volumes, London, 1922) is an informative history by apologists of the high command; *Great Britain and the War of 1914–1918* by Sir Ernest Llewelyn Woodward (London, 1967) contains a balanced but biting critique of British strategy on the Western Front. Both are eminently readable. Winston Churchill's *The World Crisis, 1911–1918* (4 volumes, London 1923–37) needs little introduction. His connection with tank development has already been noted.

Several interesting books deal with the role of tanks in the trench war. Bryan Cooper's *The Ironclads of Cambrai* (London, 1967) is exciting and well detailed. Swinton, Fuller and other tank officers have published memoirs. British mining operations have been more neglected, but Alexander Barrie's *War Underground* (London, 1962) goes a long way towards filling the gap with a fascinating text and some useful diagrams. A wider summary of engineer operations is in *Work of the R.E. in the European War 1914–1918* by the Institution of Royal Engineers (London, 1922). Equally neglected, the story of the RAMC in World War I – an extraordinary chapter in medical history – still awaits publication in substantial form. Meanwhile, Redmond McLaughlin's *The Royal Army Medical Corps* (London, 1972) provides a compelling introduction.

As a contribution to the understanding of the trench war, Martin Middlebrook's *The First Day on the Somme* (London, 1971) ranges well beyond the limits of its title, an admirably researched and narrated impression not only of the battle but of the formation and composition of Kitchener's army. Top level observations on the

Somme battles and other trench campaigns are available in Haig's *Despatches 1915–19* (London, 1919), Falkenhayn's *General Headquarters 1914–16 and its Critical Decisions* (London, 1919), Ludendorff's *My War Memories* (London, 1922), and *The Personal Memoirs of Joffre* (London, 1932).

Two books whose titles might not immediately commend them to seekers of trench war literature are *Morale* by John Baynes (London, 1967), an often provocative but illuminating thesis on regular army attitudes at the time by an author with a military background; and *Promise of Greatness*, edited by George A. Panichas (London, 1968). With a foreword by Sir Herbert Read, the latter includes a number of engrossing essays by familiar writers who were present in the trenches.

Also recommended for a variety of interest and information:

Bairnsfather, Bruce, *Bullets and Billets,* London, 1916.

Barnett, Corelli, *The Sword Bearers,* London, 1963.

Chamberlain, W. (comp.), *Industrial Relations in Wartime 1914–1918,* London, 1940.

Chapman, Guy, (ed), *Vain Glory,* London, 1937.

Edmonds, Sir James, *A Short History of World War I*, London, 1951.

Foulkes, Maj-Gen. C. H., *'Gas!'*, London, 1934.

Fradkin, E. T., *Chemical Warfare,* London, 1929.

Haig, Sir Douglas (ed. Blake, R.), *The Private Papers of Douglas Haig 1914–1919,* London, 1952.

Harbord, J. G., *The American Army in France 1917–1919,* New York and London, 1936.

Henniker, A. M., *Transportation on the Western Front 1914–1918,* London, 1937.

Kiernan, R. H., *The First War in the Air,* London, 1934.

Lutz, R. H. (ed.), *The Causes of the German Collapse in 1918,* London, 1934.

Spears, E. L., *Prelude to Victory,* London, 1939.

Thoumin, Richard (ed. and trans. Kieffer, M.), *The First World War,* London, 1963.

Tyng, S. T., *The Campaign of the Marne 1914,* London, 1935.

Index